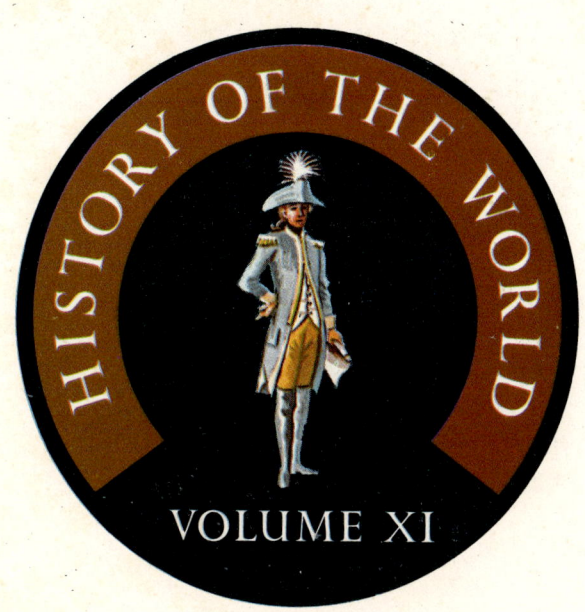

IMPORTANT DATES AND EVENTS IN

The American Revolution
1765 The British try to raise money by requiring tax stamps on documents; the colonies protest.
1766 The Stamp Act repealed.
1767 The Townshend Acts impose taxes on imported goods; unrest continues in the colonies.
1770 British troops open fire on a crowd in the Boston Massacre; The Townshend Acts repealed.
1772 A mob burns the British coast guard ship *Gaspee;* Sam Adams starts the first committee of correspondence in Boston.
1773 Boston patriots dressed as Indians destroy three shiploads of tea in the Boston Tea Party.
1774 In reprisal for the Tea Party the British blockade Boston; the first Continental Congress meets in Philadelphia to consider ways of protesting.
1775 The revolution begins as minutemen fire on British troops at Lexington and Concord; Washington becomes commander-in-chief; British win the battle of Bunker Hill but suffer heavy losses.
1776 British troops evacuate Boston;

THE AGE OF REVOLUTION 1765-1791

Congress adopts the Declaration of Independence; Washington crosses the Delaware and defeats the Hessians at Trenton.
1777 The British are defeated in battles at Princeton, Bennington and Saratoga.
1778 France enters the war on the colonists' side; Lafayette joins Washington's army.
1781 Washington and a French fleet trap Cornwallis at Yorktown; his surrender ends the war.
1783 Britain recognizes American independence by the Treaty of Paris.

The French Revolution
1787 The Assembly of Notables meets; Lafayette demands that the king call the Estates General.
1789 The Estates General meets but the Third Estate declares itself a National Assembly and begins to write a constitution; Parisians storm the Bastille, arm themselves, and force the king to return from Versailles to Paris.
1791 The king is captured while trying to flee Paris and begin a counterrevolution, and is returned to his palace in Paris.

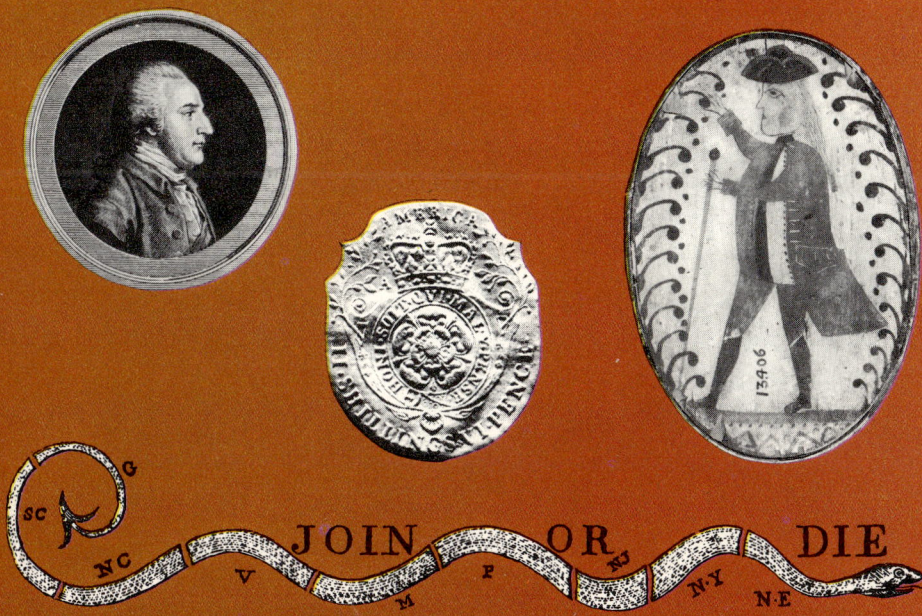

HISTORY OF

Editor   Irwin Shapiro
Associate Editor   Jonathan Bartlett
Consultant   Albert Fried,
*Department of History,
Queens College, New York*

Contributors   Anne Howard Bailey
John Bowman
Ormonde de Kay, Jr.
Edith Firoozi
Albert Fried
Johanna Johnston
Ira N. Klein
Willis Lindquist
Edna Ritchie
Seymour Reit
James L. Steffensen

VOLUME XI

THE UNIVERSAL
THE WORLD

THE AGE OF REVOLUTION

by Willis Lindquist

GOLDEN PRESS NEW YORK

CONTENTS

THE AMERICAN REVOLUTION 1765-1781

Trouble in Boston 1770   869
The Boston Massacre enrages the colonists.

England Tightens Her Grip 1763-1765   872
Parliament taxes the colonies to help pay for the French and Indian War.

The Stamp Act 1765-1772   874
The colonists' violent opposition to the Stamp Act leads to its repeal.

The Boston Tea Party 1773-1774   878
The colonists dump English tea in Boston harbor and the British blockade the port.

The Continental Congress 1774   880
Delegates from the colonies meet to oppose taxation without representation.

War Begins on Lexington Green 1775   882
Minutemen begin the revolution by firing on British troops.

England's First Victory 1775   888
The British win Breed's Hill in Boston, but suffer serious losses.

Good King George and the Dragon 1775   891
Thomas Paine rallies Americans to the cause of independence.

A Divided Country 1776   893
The British retreat from Boston, but many colonists remain loyal to the king.

© COPYRIGHT 1966 BY WESTERN PUBLISHING COMPANY, INC., AND LIBRAIRIE HACHETTE. ALL RIGHTS RESERVED INCLUDING THE RIGHT OF REPRODUCTION IN WHOLE OR IN PART IN ANY FORM. DESIGNED AND PRODUCED BY ARTISTS AND WRITERS PRESS, INC. PRINTED IN THE U.S.A. BY WESTERN PRINTING AND LITHOGRAPHING COMPANY. PUBLISHED BY GOLDEN PRESS, INC., NEW YORK.

The Final Break   1776   896
The colonies declare their independence from England.

The Old Fox   1776-1777   900
Washington's small, ill-equipped army defeats the British at Trenton and Princeton.

The Road to Yorktown   1777-1781   904
The colonists and their French allies trap Cornwallis and force him to surrender.

THE FRENCH REVOLUTION   1782-1815

Champion of Liberty   1782-1789   911
Lafayette returns from America and hopes to bring liberty to France.

The Voice of the People   1789   916
The king summons the Estates General, but the commoners rebel.

The Fall of the Bastille   1789   921
The people of Paris capture the Bastille and elect Lafayette head of the militia.

"The King to Paris!"   1789   925
Louis tries to stall the Assembly but the people bring him captive to Paris.

The Fall of King Louis   1789-1793   928
The king is executed when his plots against the revolution are discovered.

The Terror   1793-1795   934
The revolutionaries take drastic steps to put down their enemies.

The Rise of Napoleon Bonaparte   1796-1802   939
After great successes in Italy, Napoleon makes peace and becomes First Consul.

Emperor of the French   1804-1815   945
Napoleon becomes emperor but is finally defeated at Waterloo.

THE AMERICAN REVOLUTION

THE PEOPLE OF BOSTON HATED THE BRITISH TROOPS THAT OCCUPIED THEIR CITY, AND CALLED THEM "LOBSTERS" BECAUSE OF THE COLOR OF THEIR COATS.

Trouble in Boston
1770

EVEN AFTER IT HAPPENED, few people in colonial Boston knew the boy's name. He was just a barber's helper. But everyone heard about him on the night of the trouble. On that night he set off an angry mob by pointing his finger at a British guard, and the violence that followed became a famous incident in American history.

The date was March 5, 1770. Boston was then occupied by British troops. The troops had been brought in to keep order and to force the people to pay taxes they did not want to pay. The people of Boston hated the troops and insulted them at every opportunity. Boys threw snowballs at them, and called them "lobsters" because their long red coats were almost the color of boiled lobsters.

On the night of the trouble, the barber's helper started things off by calling a British officer names. He became so insulting that a British soldier on guard duty nearby finally lost his temper and struck the boy on the head with the butt of his rifle.

News of the attack spread quickly to shops and taverns. Within an hour small bands of men were roving the streets looking for trouble with the hated redcoats. They met a large band of redcoats who were also out looking for trouble.

Trouble in Boston

The badly outnumbered civilians soon took to their heels. To get more people into the streets someone rang a church bell, Boston's way of sounding the fire alarm.

People who came out of their houses to help fight the fire were told about the boy who had been struck down by a British soldier. That was too much. They searched for the barber's helper and found him. The boy repeated his story, probably exaggerating to win more sympathy from the crowd. He led them to the sentry box in front of the Customs House and, pointing to the soldier on duty there, identified him as the one who had struck the blow.

"Kill him! Kill him!" someone shouted.

The angry crowd rushed at the soldier. He held them off with his bayonet as he backed up the steps of the Customs House, calling for help. A sergeant and six guards came to his aid. They lined up in front of the mob, which by now numbered almost a hundred men, and leveled their rifles at them. The sergeant warned the people to stand back, but that only made them more furious. They advanced slowly, daring the soldiers to fire. Some began throwing snowballs, stones, sticks—anything they could lay their hands on.

As the mob closed in, a heavy stick hit a soldier named Montgomery. In anger, or by accident, Montgomery fired his rifle into the mob. A man named Crispus Attucks screamed and pitched forward on his face in the snow. In the excitement, other soldiers fired. The stunned crowd stood for a moment in horror, then fell back and scattered, leaving behind them three dead and several seriously wounded.

To prevent further bloodshed, all British soldiers in Boston were removed to Castle William, a fort in the harbor. The redcoats who had done the shooting were given a jury trial. Only two were found guilty, and they were let off with light sentences because of the threatening action of the mob.

ADAMS STIRS UP THE PEOPLE

The trial should have ended the matter, but it did not. Samuel Adams and other political leaders of Massachusetts saw to that. They used the incident to stir up the people against England. They called it the Boston Massacre, and published exaggerated reports about it. They also sent out thousands of copies of a cartoon by Paul Revere showing a line of British soldiers shooting down peaceful citizens in the street. These political leaders felt that they were doing their patriotic duty by making the Boston Massacre seem worse than it was. They thought people needed a shock to make them realize their liberty was being threatened by the mother country. They wanted to make people angry enough to stand up for their rights in the family quarrel then going on between England and her American colonies.

Chubby little Samuel Adams was doing everything he could to keep the quarrel alive. As a member of the Massachusetts legislature, he spoke out against British rule at every opportunity. He knew there were other colonists who hated the British as much as he did, but very few were doing anything about it. They needed leadership, someone who could bring them together.

SAMUEL ADAMS TOOK EVERY OPPORTUNITY TO AROUSE ANTI-BRITISH FEELING.

PAUL REVERE'S CARTOON OF THE BOSTON MASSACRE WAS WIDELY DISTRIBUTED.

Trouble in Boston

THE RESIDENTIAL STREETS OF COLONIAL NEW YORK WERE CALM AND QUIET, BUT SHIPS FROM THE BUSY PORT CARRIED ON TRADE THROUGHOUT THE WORLD.

England Tightens Her Grip
1763-1765

There had been few serious misunderstandings between the colonies and the mother country before the French and Indian War, but that was mainly because England had allowed the colonies to do pretty much as they pleased. They had been free to set up their own governments, make their own laws, have their own armed forces, print their own paper money, and manage most of their local affairs as they saw fit.

England's American colonies had enjoyed far more freedom and independence than had any of the colonies of France or Spain. Not that England planned it that way. She had merely neglected the colonies for well over a hundred years. At first she had neglected them because they were small and far away, and did not seem very im-

In New York, for example, there were many who felt that England had treated them unfairly. Among them were the manufacturers of beaver hats and woolen goods and iron articles. The English Parliament had passed laws which forced all of them out of business because they were taking too many customers away from manufacturers in England.

Many owners of large plantations in the southern colonies also bore a grudge against England. They were deeply in debt to British business firms, and blamed their money problems on British trade laws. They had to sell their cotton, tobacco, and hides in England at prices which were often unreasonably low and buy their manufactured goods in England at prices that were often very high. They saw themselves as victims of unfair trade laws, which had been forced upon them for the benefit of the mother country.

Most of those who had turned against England had done so after the end of the French and Indian War in 1763. That was the year when the family quarrel between England and her American colonies took a sudden turn for the worse.

portant. Later she had neglected them because she was busy fighting one war after another with her most serious rivals, France and Spain.

England had finally brought that struggle to an end with the great victory in the French and Indian War. It was the kind of victory she had been trying to win for seventy years. She won Florida from Spain, and Canada and the wilderness east of the Mississippi from France. On the other side of the world, England had won French possessions in India as well. Her powerful navy ruled the seas, and she was the strongest nation on earth.

At the same time, the war had left England with many problems. She was deeply in debt, yet she had to support a large navy to protect her vast empire. To provide business for her many new factories, she had to find ways of increasing her trade with the colonies. England could no longer afford to neglect her American colonies. She had to tighten her grip on them and treat them in a businesslike way, so that their strength and wealth would be of greater benefit to her.

The war had brought about changes in the American colonies, too. It had left them with a large number of trained colonial soldiers with war experience. The peace treaty had removed the threat of French armies along their borders, and they no longer had a strong need for British protection. They felt that they had at last reached the point where they could take care of themselves. They wanted more freedom, not less; fewer controls, not more. Thus England began tightening her grip at the very time the colonies were searching for ways to loosen some of their ties with the mother country.

England already had laws requiring the colonies to do most of their trading with the mother country. To discourage trade with other countries, high taxes had been placed on goods imported from foreign lands. But these laws had never been strictly enforced, and for many years the colonists had been able to avoid high import taxes by smuggling in whatever they wanted to buy from foreign countries. Smuggling had become a standard practice, and many of the most respected businessmen in the colonies—men like John Hancock—had made their fortunes in this way.

Now, to enforce her trade laws and prevent smuggling, England encouraged her officers to use Writs of Assistance. The writs were papers which allowed British officials to enter ships, warehouses, and other buildings in search of smuggled goods. A young Boston lawyer named James Otis won fame by carrying the fight against such writs to the courts. He pointed out in his speech to the jury that Writs of Assistance could be used to enter and search private homes. This

KING GEORGE III

denied the colonists one of their most precious rights as Englishmen, the right to live undisturbed in their own homes. Although Otis lost the case, he continued fighting for the rights of colonial Englishmen.

England's enforcement of the trade laws brought heavy losses to John Hancock and thousands of other smugglers. Many of them had to give up smuggling altogether. Some became so bitter toward England that they joined radical groups and did what they could to encourage rebellion against the mother country.

The Stamp Act
1765-1772

Another unpopular step England took after the war was to reorganize her defense system in the colonies. The French and Indian War had proved to the British that the colonies could not be depended upon to defend themselves. Some new system had to be worked out in North America, to defend not only the colonies, but also Canada, Florida, and the wilderness east of the Mississippi. England decided to leave this task to a standing army of ten thousand British redcoats.

Such an army would cost a great deal of money. Taxpayers in England were already paying very high taxes, and could not be asked to pay more. Their taxes supported the powerful British navy, which protected the colonies as well as the mother country. It seemed no more than fair that the colonies should pay at least part of the expenses of the standing army in North America. The soldiers were there, after all, for their own protection.

Accordingly, the colonies were given a year to raise the money themselves. They were warned that England would have to tax them if they failed to do so. For a year the colonists did nothing. They saw no need of supporting an army they had not asked for and did not want. Since the French forces had been driven from American soil, a large standing army seemed unnecessary. The colonists suspected that the real purpose

THE COLONISTS PARADED TO PROTEST AGAINST PARLIAMENT'S STAMP ACT.

of the army was to strengthen British control over all the colonial governments.

England's law-making body in London, the British Parliament, finally passed the Stamp Act in 1765. It required the colonists to buy stamps from British tax collectors. These stamps were to be placed on all newspapers, playing cards, dice, and almanacs sold in the colonies, and also on certain papers having to do with business and law.

Political leaders in the colonies cried out against the tax. They pointed out that England had never before taxed anything within the borders of the colonies. In the Virginia assembly, a new member from the backwoods country, Patrick Henry, made an angry speech in which he said that Virginians did not have to pay any taxes except those of their own colonial government. A short time later, a Stamp Act congress was held in New York, to which nine colonies sent representatives. The congress declared that only the colonial legislatures had the power to tax Americans.

The Stamp Act

An organization known as the Sons of Liberty was formed to fight the tax. Its members argued that taxation without representation was wrong. And since the colonies were not represented in Parliament, Parliament had no right to tax them. The Sons of Liberty held parades and mass meetings to stir up public feeling. They threatened the tax collectors who sold the stamps, and forced many of them to resign. Sometimes mobs broke into the homes of tax collectors, smashed furniture, and burned piles of stamps in the street.

Benjamin Franklin of Philadelphia was in London at the time as an agent of the colony of Pennsylvania. He was called before Parliament and asked, "Do you think it right that America should be protected by this country and pay no part of the expenses?"

Franklin answered, "That is not the case. The colonies raised, clothed, and paid during the war twenty-five thousand men, and spent many millions."

He was asked whether Americans would consent to a stamp tax if the tax rate were lower.

"No," said Franklin, "they would never submit to it."

Franklin proved to be right. Many colonists decided to "eat nothing, drink nothing, wear nothing" imported from England until Parliament did away with the hated stamp tax. This was a serious blow to British manufacturers. Worried by their business losses, they demanded that Parliament do something about the tax.

THE STAMP ACT REPEALED

And so the stamp tax became an important political question in England itself. Members of Parliament who did not belong to the political party then in control of the government saw that here was a chance to strike at their opponents. They supported William Pitt, who said, "The Americans are the sons of England. As subjects they are entitled to the common right of representation and cannot be bound to pay taxes without their consent."

AFTER THE STAMP ACT'S REPEAL, THIS BRITISH PRINT DEPICTED ITS "FUNERAL."

875

After much bitter argument, Parliament finally did away with the stamp tax in March of 1766. The colonists were so pleased with their victory they closed up their places of business for a day of celebration. But they were still unhappy about the large standing army and the Quartering Act, which required all colonists with vacant houses and barns to make them available as living quarters for British troops whenever necessary. Americans did not like being forced to keep British troops on their private property.

TOWNSHEND AND TAXES

To make matters worse, Britain soon came up with another scheme to solve her serious money problems. Charles Townshend, a new minister in the king's cabinet, believed the colonies had been against the stamp tax mainly because it was collected within the colonies. He felt the Americans would not object to import taxes, which would be collected at the borders. He persuaded Parliament to pass the Townshend Acts, which placed taxes on all lead, glass, paints, tea, and paper imported by the colonies. Furthermore, anyone caught smuggling could be tried without a jury. The British believed in trial by jury, but they knew from past experience that colonial juries looked upon smugglers as heroes and refused to find them guilty. The only practical way of punishing smugglers, therefore, was to try them without juries. But the colonists were very much concerned that their rights, as Englishmen, to trial by jury were now being taken from them. Why, they were being treated as if they were no longer free men!

Leading citizens in every colony quickly joined the fight against the Townshend Acts. They pointed out that the old import taxes of the trade laws had been passed to discourage the buying of goods from other lands. That had been legal, they said, because Parliament had the right to regulate foreign trade. But it did not have the right to pass import taxes for the purpose of raising money. Colonial merchants in the North and some in the South stopped buying goods from England. In Virginia, George Washington and other plantation owners organized a group who agreed to stop buying goods from England so long as the Townshend Acts remained in force.

At the suggestion of Samuel Adams, the Massachusetts assembly wrote letters to other colonial assemblies, asking them all to join in the fight against the Townshend Acts. People in Boston treated the tax collectors so badly that many of them feared for their lives. British troops were brought into the city to protect them and to restore order. Then came the night of the Boston Massacre. The bloodstains on the snow soon disappeared, but Samuel Adams never let the people forget that British redcoats had shot down unarmed citizens in the street. Through his efforts the Boston Massacre brought the colonies one step closer to open revolt, and also helped bring about the repeal of the Townshend Acts later that year.

All the import taxes were repealed except for the one on tea—and the colonists were able to avoid that by smuggling in tea from Holland. The next two years were peaceful. Business conditions improved, and most people were so pleased with their lot that they were beginning to look upon Samuel Adams and his kind as radicals and troublemakers.

In Providence, Rhode Island, long an important smuggling center, almost everyone was benefiting directly or indirectly from the business of smuggling tax-free tea from Holland. Then the British sent the coast guard schooner *Gaspee*, commanded by Lieutenant Dudingston, to make war on smugglers along the broken coast of Rhode Island. Dudingston did his work so well that he soon became the most unpopular man in Providence. But on the evening of June 8, 1772, the *Gaspee* ran aground in the shallows off Point Namquit, and the people of Providence had a chance to strike back. After a drummer had gone about the town announcing that the *Gaspee* was helplessly aground, a large number of people gathered at Sabin's tavern in the center of town. There they molded bullets in the kitchen, loaded their guns, and planned their attack. Presently they set out in rowboats for the grounded schooner seven miles to the south.

Some time later, they caught sight of the masts of the *Gaspee* looming tall and dark against the sky. They approached quietly. Just as they were about to board the ship, a cry came from the deck. The men of Providence answered it with a few musket shots and swarmed up over the side. Dudingston and his crew were taken completely by surprise. They were rowed to a small rocky island nearby and left stranded there, while the *Gaspee* was set afire. Flames leaped from the

COLONIALS FROM PROVIDENCE ROWED OUT TO THE GROUNDED BRITISH COAST GUARD SCHOONER *GASPEE* AND BURNED IT TO THE WATERLINE.

vessel, sparks swirled into the night sky, and by morning it had burned to its water line.

The British were enraged. They sent investigators to Providence to arrest the raiders and to bring them to London for trial. But no arrests were ever made. No one in Providence seemed to be able to identify even a single raider.

Samuel Adams smiled when he heard the news of the *Gaspee.* For the most part, though, Americans were too contented to suit him. There was little he could do about it until a report came from London that England was planning to pay the salaries of colonial governors out of money collected from import taxes. This meant that the colonial assemblies, which had previously paid the salaries of the king's appointed governors, would no longer be able to control the governors by threatening to withhold their salaries. Adams warned that if the governors were paid directly by England, they would rule over the colonies as they pleased. The time had come, he said, when the people had to decide whether they were to be "freemen or slaves."

At a Boston town meeting in November, 1772, Samuel Adams, his second cousin John Adams, James Otis, and other leaders re-organized the

PATRIOTS DRESSED AS INDIANS DUMPED THREE SHIPLOADS OF TEA INTO THE HARBOR IN THE BOSTON TEA PARTY.

Committee of Correspondence. The committee had been set up to exchange political information and views with other colonists. Soon more than eighty towns in Massachusetts had formed similar committees. In Virginia, the legislature appointed a Committee of Correspondence, and most of the other colonies soon followed her example. The committees united the colonies and stirred up public opinion against England.

The Boston Tea Party
1773-1774

Because of the tax on tea, many of the colonists began drinking coffee or cocoa, or bought tea smuggled in from Holland. Within a few years, the British tea trade with the colonies dropped from 900,000 pounds to 237,000 pounds, and in England the warehouses of the East India Company were filled to overflowing.

The East India Company was Britain's largest and most important trading company, and to save it, Parliament passed the Tea Act. The East India Company was given a monopoly on tea trade with the colonies—that is, it was the only company allowed to sell tea to the Americans. It was also permitted to sell its tea through its agents directly to retail stores. This plan would cut out the profit made by British and American shippers and importers. Even after the tax had been paid, the British tea could be sold in the colonies at a price far below that of smuggled tea.

The British believed they had hit upon the perfect way to solve the troublesome tea problem. The colonists would rush to buy tea at a low price, the East India Company would be saved, the government would collect its tax, and everyone would be happy. To the surprise of the British, nothing of the sort happened. The Americans were angrier than ever. The merchants feared that if the direct-selling plan of the Tea Act was successful, England would decide to sell other goods in the same way, and many businessmen would be ruined. It was clear, too, that England had deliberately kept the tax on tea to show that Parliament had the right to tax colonial imports for the purpose of raising money. Leading American lawyers denied that Parliament had such a right. An import tax on low-priced tea was just as wrong as the import tax on expensive tea had been under the Townshend Act.

In several American cities, the colonists turned back ships carrying British tea, or would not allow the tea to be sold after it was landed. In Boston, Samuel Adams saw that here was another chance to stir up feeling against England. When three ships loaded with tea sailed into Boston Harbor, he called a meeting at the Old South Meeting House. Hundreds of people gathered there on the afternoon of December 16, 1773, and they decided not to allow the ships to land their cargoes. They waited while one of the ship owners went to get permission from Governor Hutchinson for the ships to leave.

Darkness had already fallen before the ship owner returned. He announced that the governor would not allow the ships to leave until the tea

tax had been paid. A hush fell over the crowd, and Samuel Adams slowly rose to his feet.

"This meeting," he said, "can do nothing more to save the country."

Everyone understood what he meant. The time had come for action—and they were ready. From the back of the meeting house came a sound like an Indian warwhoop. Someone shouted, "The Mohawks are come!" Another voice cried out, "To Griffin's Wharf!"

A number of men dressed as Indians appeared at the door of the meeting house, shouting and waving hatchets. Followed by the crowd, they hurried to the docks, where they boarded the tea ships. They broke open the holds, chopped the tea chests open and dumped the tea into the harbor. In three hours the job was finished, and the sweet smell of wet tea filled the air.

The British were shocked and angered by the Boston Tea Party, as it came to be called. The colonists were trying to force them to back down on the Tea Act. The destruction of the tea was a challenge to British authority. Americans must be made to understand that it was not up to them to decide which laws of England they would obey and which they would not. One member of Parliament declared that "it would be best to blow the town of Boston about the ears of its inhabitants," and that a hundred or so of the rebels should be hanged to set an example.

After much debate, Parliament decided to punish the rebels by taking away some of the powers of their colonial assembly. General Gage was appointed governor, and more British troops were sent to Boston to keep order. The British also slapped a blockade on the Port of Boston. No ships would be allowed to enter or leave until the people had paid for every leaf of tea.

BOSTON UNDER BLOCKADE

The blockade of Boston was a serious matter, but the city did not suffer for lack of food. Flocks of sheep were driven there from Connecticut and from Brooklyn. The people of New York promised to supply enough food for ten years if necessary. Corn was sent from Virginia, rice from South Carolina. Barrels of flour came from Philadelphia, and fish from nearby villages.

What disturbed the Americans most was the British attempt to cut down the power of the colonial government in Massachusetts by placing limits on the colonial assembly. If the British could make changes in colonial governments, they also had the power to destroy those governments. The Committees of Correspondence in Boston pointed this out to other colonies, and warned that a blow struck against one colony was really a blow against them all. It said that England was waging war against American freedom. Committees in other colonies took up the fight and sent messages to each other by express riders mounted on swift horses. A young man in the Virginia assembly, named Thomas Jefferson, called for a day of fasting and prayer to unite the people against any threat to American rights. Another Virginian, George Washington, said that the question was whether Americans would sit quietly and do nothing while one colony after another was being reduced to slavery.

The colonists soon realized they could better protect their rights if they had some central authority. On June 17, 1774, at the suggestion of Samuel Adams, the Massachusetts assembly proposed that a Continental Congress be held in Philadelphia the following September.

Samuel Adams was chosen as one of the delegates from Massachusetts. But he had spent so much of his time fighting the British that he was almost penniless, and his clothes were too shabby to wear to the congress. One evening, he was surprised by a visit from a tailor, who came to measure him for a suit. Next came a shirtmaker, then a hatter, and then a shoemaker. A few days later, a trunk arrived at his house. In it were a suit of clothes, a cloak, a cocked hat, stylish shoes with silver buckles, and a gold-headed cane. They had been paid for by his friends.

THOMAS JEFFERSON

The Continental Congress
1774

When Samuel Adams, his cousin John Adams, and the rest of the delegates from Massachusetts arrived in Philadelphia, they found themselves very unpopular. Cousin John complained that he was avoided as if he had some sort of contagious disease. The delegates from other colonies looked upon the men from Massachusetts as radicals, and did not like their wild ideas about protecting American rights with force, if necessary.

But Patrick Henry of Virginia made a speech pointing out that it was no longer possible for any of the colonies to stand alone. They had to unite, to work together with other colonies for the good of all. "I am not a Virginian," he cried, "but an American!"

Most of the delegates to the Congress were still loyal to the king, but, like Patrick Henry, they had begun to think of themselves as Americans rather than Englishmen. More and more, they were speaking of justice and freedom and liberty, and of the natural rights of man. And one of the first things they did was to write a Declaration of Rights, describing exactly what rights they claimed for themselves.

The colonists, declared the Congress, were "entitled to life, liberty, and property," and had never given any "foreign power" authority to change, or to take away, any of those rights without consent. The Congress also stated that it was the right of Englishmen and of all free people to govern themselves. Since the colonists were not represented in the British Parliament, they were entitled to have their own law-making bodies. The colonial legislatures were the only law-making bodies that had authority to tax and to make laws for the various colonies. At the same time, the Congress recognized the right of the king to veto laws passed by the legislatures.

The Congress also passed a plan known as the Association. It provided that the people of all

880

the colonies were to stop trading with England until the Port of Boston was opened again. The names of those who did trade with the British were to be published in the newspapers. Some of the worst offenders were later whipped in public, or tarred and feathered. Local committees enforced the Association plan so well that, within a year after the meeting of the First Continental Congress, imports from England had almost stopped.

But the big issue raised by the Congress was the right of Parliament to pass laws for the colonies, or to make them pay taxes. The British insisted that Parliament was the law-making body for the entire empire. Its members represented the people of the colonies as well as those of England, and therefore it had as much right to pass laws for the colonies as it did to pass laws for England.

It was difficult for the ordinary Englishman to understand why the colonists were making such a big fuss about not being represented in Parliament. The great majority of Englishmen had never had a chance to vote for a member of Parliament. That right was limited to the nobility and to property owners in the upper classes. Furthermore, some of the new factory towns in England had no one in Parliament to represent them. So it seemed to the average Englishman that the colonists were being unreasonable. By insisting on the right to be represented, they were demanding something that even most Englishmen in England did not have.

KING AND PARLIAMENT

The colonists pointed out that the colonies had received their charters and their right to set up local governments directly from the king, not from Parliament. England and the colonies had the same king, but he was the only connecting link between them. The colonists argued that Parliament was the law-making body for England, just as the colonial assemblies were the law-making bodies for the colonies. Each colony, therefore, had a little parliament of its own. The British Parliament, they insisted, had no more right to pass laws for Massachusetts than the little parliament in Massachusetts had to pass laws for England. The colonists also claimed they were willing to pay their fair share of the expenses of the empire. The king, they said, could always

THE FIRST CONTINENTAL CONGRESS MET IN THE STATE HOUSE IN PHILADELPHIA.

request the colonial assemblies to raise needed funds through their own taxing powers.

But England had already tried this method during the French and Indian War, with poor results. Some colonies had refused to pay anything, while others had paid only a small portion of their share. Every now and then through the years various people had suggested a simple solution to the whole question of Parliament's power to tax. All that was needed, they said, was to give each of the colonies the right to be represented in the British Parliament. Then no one in America could deny the right of Parliament to tax them. The colonists opposed the idea. Their representatives in Parliament would be so few in number that the British members could easily outvote them. The British were also against the idea. The colonies were growing rapidly, but England itself was not. If all the people of the empire were to be represented, the time would come when there would be more American representatives in Parliament than there were British. The British did not like the idea of being ruled by America any more than the Americans liked being ruled by the British.

War Begins on Lexington Green

1775

On the evening of April 18, 1775, Paul Revere quietly made his way through the dark streets of Boston to the Charles River. At the river's edge he hid in the shadows, watching and waiting. He kept a sharp lookout for British patrols. Spies had brought the patriots word that the British were to launch a surprise attack; Revere, William Dawes, and other members of the Sons of Liberty had made careful plans to warn the countryside.

There could be no doubt that something was about to happen. Several days earlier, eight hundred of the best troops stationed in Boston had been taken off regular duty to prepare for action of some sort. According to the spies, General Gage had become alarmed at the way the colonists in every village were drilling and gathering military supplies. He was particularly concerned about the large supply of ammunition that the colonists had stored at Concord, some twenty miles from Boston. And he was anxious to arrest Samuel Adams and John Hancock, who were spending a few days in Lexington at the home of Reverend Jonas Clark.

PAUL REVERE'S RIDE

Now a number of British patrols had been sent out on the roads leading to Lexington and Concord, so the patriots were certain that their information was correct. The British intended to arrest Adams and Hancock in Lexington, and then go on to destroy the ammunition at Concord. But which way would the British go? Boston was located on a peninsula, connected with the mainland by a narrow neck of land. The British might go over the neck, through Roxbury and Cambridge. That was the long way. They could cut off a number of miles by crossing the Charles River on boats.

It was about ten o'clock when Paul Revere heard the sounds of marching men. The British were on the move. He watched until he saw them take to the boats at Park Square. That was all he needed to know. He hurried to the North Church and told the man waiting there to hang two lanterns in the church tower, a signal to William Dawes and others that the British were going by water. Revere quickly returned to the waterfront, rowed across the river some distance from where the British were crossing, and mounted a fast horse held ready for him on the other side. Meanwhile, Revere knew, William Dawes was riding the long way, through Cambridge. If one of them should get caught by a British patrol, the other might be able to get through and carry the alarm to Lexington and Concord. Other riders would fan out to alert the volunteer soldiers, called minutemen because they were ready to serve at a minute's notice.

THE AMERICAN REVOLUTION BEGAN WITH THE FIGHTING ON LEXINGTON GREEN.

Revere set out at a gallop. "In Bedford," he said later, "I awaked the captain and the minutemen and after that I alarmed almost every house till I got to Lexington."

Just before dawn, he reached Lexington. The church bell sounded the warning that everyone had been expecting, and farmers armed with flintlocks began gathering on the village green opposite the white Congregational Church. At Parson Clark's house, Paul Revere reported to his friends Adams and Hancock. They were preparing to leave when Dawes came galloping up.

Revere and Dawes rode off together to warn the people of Concord. They had gone only a few miles when their way was suddenly blocked by a British patrol on horses. Dawes managed to slip by and continued on to Concord. Revere was caught and questioned, and was forced to return to Lexington on foot.

By the time the first rays of sun flooded Lexington green, most of the farmers in the neighborhood had gathered there, about seventy in all, under the command of Captain John Parker. From the distance came the music of fifes and drums. The music grew louder as the British marched into view over the crest of the hill on the road from Boston. The troops in the long column looked like toy soldiers, all in bright red and white, all marching briskly in perfect order. On they came, as if nothing could stop them, with Major Pitcairn riding ahead. Eight hundred experienced troops of the King's army—what could less than a hundred untrained farmers with muskets hope to do against them?

"DISPERSE, YE REBELS!"

Captain Parker, who led the minutemen, seemed to be a little uncertain about it himself. He had been instructed to gather his men on the green, but no one had told him what to do next. "Let the troops pass," he told his men.

As the redcoats came marching up, Major Pit-

883

cairn cried out, "Disperse, ye rebels! Lay down your arms and disperse!"

Captain Parker quickly ordered his minutemen to stay where they were. "Don't fire unless fired upon; but if they mean to have war, let it begin here."

For several moments nothing happened. Then a sharp report of a gun broke the stillness. No one ever knew who fired the shot, but it marked the beginning of the American Revolution.

The redcoats, certain that the shot had come from the American ranks, replied with a hail of bullets. Major Pitcairn drew his sword and rode back and forth in front of his men, trying to make them stop firing, but they "were so wild they could hear no orders." The patriots returned their fire, then scattered and took up positions behind houses, stone walls, and trees.

Major Pitcairn finally regained control of his men. The shooting stopped. The smoke cleared from the green, revealing the bodies of eight dead minutemen, and several wounded. On the British side, one of the redcoats and a horse were slightly wounded.

BATTLE AT THE BRIDGE

The British set off for Concord without bothering to search the village for Adams and Hancock. But they need not have been in a hurry. Most of the military supplies stored in Concord had already been removed by patriots and hidden in other places.

When the British arrived in Concord, they spent several hours in a house-to-house search of the village. They were polite and very proper in their conduct. At one house, an officer asked why the door to one of the rooms was locked. He was told that it was occupied by a sick person who wasn't to be disturbed. He accepted this explanation and went away without knowing that the room was actually a storage place for military supplies. While the search was going on, three companies of light infantry stood guard at the North Bridge on the edge of town. Four other companies passed over the bridge to search the farm of Colonel Barrett a mile out of town.

All this time patriots from nearby villages were gathering in the hills beyond Concord. There was no one to take command. They talked things over and wondered what to do. A number of them formed a column of two's and marched down the hill directly toward North Bridge. The British on the other side of the bridge opened fire. The minutemen scattered, took cover, and aimed carefully. So deadly was their fire that the redcoats suddenly broke ranks and fled back to the village, leaving their dead and wounded behind.

The patriots had won the bridge, but did not know what to do with it, and they went into the hills again to talk things over. They were still there, some time later, when four companies of redcoats came marching back toward the bridge after searching the Barrett farm. Although the Americans probably outnumbered the redcoats by three to one, the British were allowed to pass without a shot being fired.

Many new units of minutemen joined the others in the hills during the morning hours. Some of the men had been up since dawn. Tired and hungry, they prepared to leave for their homes. They did not think of themselves as being at war. They had not come out to defeat an enemy in battle, but rather to prove to the British that they were prepared to fight for their rights. But those who were starting for home suddenly changed their minds when they saw a dark column of smoke rising from the town of Concord.

The British were merely burning some wooden gun carriages they had found, but the patriots did not know that. They thought the British were burning the entire village. Although they still had no plan of action, the angry minutemen lingered. At noon they saw the British marching toward Lexington. They followed behind, as if to make certain the redcoats were really leaving the countryside.

There was no shooting. The British might have returned safely to Boston had it not been for a little bridge over the Mill Brook. The narrow bridge acted as a bottleneck, slowing the British down. The rear guard became nervous. They suddenly wheeled and fired at the minutemen, probably trying to keep them at a safe distance.

To the angry minutemen the reports of the British rifles were like a command to open fire. They no longer had any reason for holding back.

THE BRITISH GUARDING NORTH BRIDGE BROKE RANKS AND RAN FROM THE DEADLY ACCURATE FIRE OF THE MINUTEMEN.

Closing in on both sides of the road and from the rear, they cut the tail end of the British army to bits in a deadly crossfire.

The patriots then swarmed over the brook to continue their attack from both sides of the road. They fought Indian style, firing at the marching redcoats from behind trees, rocks, houses, and stone fences. The British light infantry units moved out on both sides to come up behind the Americans. This took some of the pressure off the main body of soldiers, but it was not enough. The road behind them was dotted with fallen redcoats. The column moved faster. As their ranks thinned out, the British began to show signs of panic. One of them, writing about it later, said, "when we arrived a mile from Lexington, our ammunition began to fail and . . . we began to run rather than retreat in order. . . ."

Some of them dropped their packs and rifles as they fled down the long slope into Lexington. They could not have gone on much longer, but in Lexington they were met by over a thousand fresh redcoats and several small cannon under the command of Major General Percy. Pitcairn's men were so exhausted that they fell to the ground with "their tongues hanging from their mouths, like those of dogs after a chase."

CAMPFIRES IN THE NIGHT

After a short rest on the village green, they set out for Boston. The rebels closed in once more, and the running battle continued. By now the whole countryside was up in arms, and new units of minutemen joined in the fight, more than making up for those who dropped out as they ran out of ammunition. The strain was too much for many of the British. They broke ranks, looted and burned houses along the road that served as snipers' nests, and shot at any civilian they saw. When their march ended in Boston late that night, they had lost seventy-two killed, 174 wounded, and twenty-six missing. Losses on the colonial side were forty-three dead, forty-nine wounded, and five missing.

The war had begun at last. And in the hills and wooded areas surrounding Boston, the twinkling lights of hundreds of colonial campfires burned through the night. The campfires rapidly increased in number as patriots from all over New England gathered to keep the British hemmed in at Boston. The news of Lexington convinced many Americans that they would now have to fight for their liberty. The colonists began making preparations for war in earnest. One newspaperman wrote, "Travel through whatever part of this country you will, you see the inhabitants training, making firelocks, casting mortars, shells and shot . . ." The most popular music in Maryland was that of the fife and drum. It became fashionable in Virginia to carry tomahawks and to wear frontiersman's hunting shirts.

THE GREEN MOUNTAIN BOYS

The Second Continental Congress met in Philadelphia on May 10, just three weeks after the battle at Lexington. The delegates were welcomed by smartly dressed companies of riflemen who guided them into the city. Most of the delegates were uneasy about the violence at Lexington. They still hoped something could be done to prevent war. So long as there was a chance to win back the liberty they had once enjoyed under the British Crown, they did not want to speak of independence. Benjamin Franklin went so far as to say, "I have never heard in any conversation from any person the least expression of a wish for independence. The Americans have too much love for their country."

Many delegates feared that the fighting at Lexington would lead to other battles unless they acted quickly. They sent an appeal to King George, saying that they were still his loyal subjects. All they were asking him to do was to restore their liberties so that England and her American colonies could live in peace and harmony once again.

A few days later they learned that Ethan Allen and his militia from New Hampshire, known as the Green Mountain Boys, had captured the British Fort of Ticonderoga on Lake Champlain. Allen had taken the fort because its cannon and ammunition were badly needed by the army of New Englanders to drive the British out of Boston. The fort was considered important to the colonists for still another reason. It controlled the only inland waterway between the colonies and Canada.

The delegates were stunned by the news. The

War Begins on Lexington Green

FORT TICONDEROGA

colonial victory had come at the very time they were appealing to the king for peace. Some suggested that the fort be returned to the British with an apology. Should they let the hot-headed New Englanders drag them all into war?

Questions of that kind troubled John Adams of Massachusetts. If the colonies were divided against each other, they would all be lost. He rose and told the Congress that England would undoubtedly strengthen her army in Boston. In

887

time that army would become strong enough to defeat the colonial army surrounding the city. Where would it go, he asked, when it had crushed all resistance in New England? Yes, it would head southward, striking at other colonies one by one, for they were all guilty of resisting British authority.

Who could stop the British from sweeping over the land? None of the colonies had strength enough to do it alone, he warned. But together they could do it. He suggested that Congress set up a Grand American Army supported by all the colonies. Congress could start such an army by taking over the New England army now encamped on the outskirts of Boston.

Who would command the American army? John Adams confessed that he had been doing some thinking about that, too. The man he had in mind was "a gentleman whose skill as an officer, whose independent fortune, great talents, and universal character would command the respect of America. . . ." That man was "a gentleman from Virginia who is among us here . . ."

GENERAL WASHINGTON

At this point, George Washington, who realized that Adams was about to mention his name, quietly rose and left the chamber.

Adams had still another reason for recommending Washington, which he told his friends in private. Washington came from the South. If the army had a commander from the South, it would help bind the colonies closer together.

Two days later, Washington was appointed "General and Commander-in-Chief of the forces raised and to be raised in the defense of American liberty." He left Philadelphia almost at once to take command of the colonial army near Boston. Even then he had no thought of leading a fight for independence. "I am well satisfied that no such thing as independence is desired by any thinking man in all North America." he wrote.

Congress began organizing the country for war, not with independence in mind, but to defend American liberty. It made plans to build a navy, to gain the friendship of the Indians, to print its own paper money, and to establish a national postal system. In taking these steps, Congress was acting like the legislative body of a nation which had already won its freedom.

England's First Victory

1775

The British in Boston had no reason for suspecting anything unusual on the night of June 16, 1775. But across the Charles River, a column of colonial soldiers was moving quietly toward the twin hills overlooking the town. Behind the soldiers came wagons loaded with picks and shovels. The grass-covered hills they were ap-

England's First Victory

proaching served as pastures, one owned by a Mr. Bunker, and the other by a Mr. Breed.

Washington had already been elected commander by the Congress in Philadelphia, but the news had not yet reached Boston, and the colonial forces knew nothing about it. Their colonial high command had given the order that Bunker's hill was to be fortified. By some mistake, the troops were instead led up Breed's hill, which was closer to the water, and just across the river from Boston.

The men began digging. From the top of the hill they could look down on the lighted windows of Boston, and could make out the dark hulls of British warships lying at anchor in the harbor. If they could fortify the hill with a few cannon, they would have Boston and the ships in the harbor at their mercy, and the British would be forced to leave the city.

Colonel William Prescott and the other officers gave their commands in whispers. There was no moon. No one was allowed to smoke. The troops dug in silence. Some made trenches, some stacked hay behind a rail fence that ran down the slope to the water's edge, and some threw up walls of fresh earth and sod and stone.

At dawn the following morning, British sentries were amazed to discover the activity on Breed's hill, and the long breastwork of freshly turned earth that crowned its top. After General Gage met with Sir William Howe and other generals who had just arrived from England, the British began firing their cannon at Breed's hill. Most of the round shot thudded harmlessly into the side of the hill, short of the mark. All the while, the colonial troops at the top kept working desperately, making ready for the battle that was sure to come.

IN ORDERLY FORMATION, THE BRITISH MARCHED UP BREED'S HILL.

889

HOWE'S TROOPS TOOK BREED'S HILL, BUT ONLY AFTER STAGGERING LOSSES.

"THE WHITES OF THEIR EYES"

It was afternoon before the redcoats crossed the river in barges and whaleboats manned by sailors from the men-of-war. From church spires and rooftops, the people of Boston watched to see the excitement. The British could easily have trapped the Americans by landing on the narrow neck of land which connected the twin hills with the mainland. But it would have taken several days to starve out the Americans, and General Howe chose to attack from the front of the hill. British pride had been hurt by the ragged retreat from Lexington. Now they had a chance for a quick and glorious victory, a chance to prove what the might of the British army could really do in face-to-face battle with untrained rebels.

At three o'clock the British formed three long scarlet lines, one behind the other, across the foot of the hill. The hot sun beat down and fluffy white clouds floated lazily overhead as the rolling of drums gave the signal for the attack. There were rail fences on the rolling slope, and knee-high grass, and clumps of thorny bushes. Even so, the redcoats managed to keep their lines straight. Each was loaded with a knapsack, blankets, three days' supply of food, ammunition, and rifle—about one hundred and twenty pounds of equipment in all.

At the top of the hill, the patriots waited behind their breastwork of earth and stone, with their best marksmen lined up in firing position.

Others crouched behind them, ready to hand up loaded muskets as fast as they could be fired. According to legend, the patriots were told to hold their fire until they could see "the whites of their eyes." Officers kept reminding the colonials that they were low on ammunition, and that they could not afford to waste a single shot.

The British came on, their rifles lowered, sun flashing on the steel of their bayonets. They had come within fifteen paces when suddenly a living wall of flame and smoke leaped from the breastwork. Hats flew in the air. Redcoats sank to the ground. Their lines crumbled. Through the dark swirl of gunsmoke the American sharpshooters kept up a constant fire. The British fell back, then turned and fled down the slope in panic.

AN EMPTY VICTORY

General Howe sent for more troops from Boston. When they arrived, he stormed the slope again. Once more they were driven back, leaving dead and wounded scattered over the hill. By now the Americans had used up most of their ammunition. Anxiously they watched as Howe massed his troops near the water for still another try. This time the redcoats staggered slowly up the slope in uneven lines. All they had left to go on was raw courage.

The patriots fired their last shots. The British reeled, but stumbled on through the smoke. They charged over the breastwork. Swords flashed. Bayonets jabbed. The Americans fought back with stones or used their rifles as clubs, trying to delay the redcoats while most of their comrades made their escape down the back side of the hill.

The Battle of Bunker Hill, as it was called, gave England her first victory over the Americans. But the victory cost her 1,054 killed and wounded, including every member of General Howe's staff that took part in the battle. The Americans lost 441 killed or wounded, and most of these were lost during the last moments of battle. They were proud of the way they had fought, and were sure they would have won if they had not run out of ammunition. "I wish we could sell them another hill at the same price," said one of them. In England, people were shocked by the heavy British losses. They joked bitterly about it, saying that if they won another such victory, there would be no one left to carry the good news back to England.

Good King George and the Dragon

1775

Samuel Adams was an unhappy man. He moved among the other delegates to Congress like a lonely, silent shadow, keeping his thoughts to himself. He dared not open his mouth for fear of saying too much.

Months had passed since the Battle of Bunker Hill. Colonial troops had made an unsuccessful attempt to drive the British from Canada. Congress had organized the Committee of Secret Correspondence to find out what help to expect from European countries in their war with England. In December of 1775, Congress had ordered the building of an American navy. Yet, in spite of all these warlike activities, Samuel Adams and other radicals did not dare speak openly about independence.

It was not fear of England that kept them silent. They were already marked men, and knew they would all probably hang if they fell into British hands. They were afraid the cause of freedom might be harmed if they spoke out too soon. They knew that most Americans were not yet ready to break away from the British Empire.

One of the most serious obstacles to independence was the people's feeling about King George. The colonists not only remained loyal to him, but believed him to be innocent of any wrongdoing.

The radicals themselves were largely to blame. They had always been careful not to say anything critical about the king. They had believed that they could more effectively stir up public opinion against Parliament if they also proved their loyalty by praising King George at the same time. Now they did not dare to speak out against the king for fear of offending the people. The false picture of a saintly king had to be destroyed before the people would be willing to fight for independence, but Samuel Adams and other radical leaders did not know how to go about it.

THE ROYAL BRUTE

Fortunately, Thomas Paine did the job for them by telling the truth about the king, as he saw it, in his famous pamphlet *Common Sense*. Paine had come from England two years before and had settled in Philadelphia. He found the Americans to be a very confused people. They did not seem to know what they were fighting for. He believed the colonies would never win their fight for liberty so long as they kept searching for it within the British Empire. England would not change, he warned. She would continue to use the colonies for her own benefit. What Americans needed was free trade in world markets, and that they could never enjoy under the British flag.

Paine urged writers and colonial leaders to give the people something worth fighting for. The only worthy cause for America was independence, he said. There had been too much confusion, too much delay. The time had come to act. The decision had to be made now. Americans had to decide whether they would face bullets and cold steel in a war of independence, or give up all thought of freedom and remain slaves of the British Crown.

What amazed Paine most of all was that Americans believed in a fairy-tale king. Paine explained that he had worked for the British government in England and knew how it operated. He said it was nonsense to believe that there was any difference between the king and his ministers, or between the king and Parliament. The truth, he said, was that the king and Parliament were working together to crush the spirit of freedom in America. The king, far from being the innocent victim of his wicked ministers, was their absolute master. He could hire and fire them at will. He was the supreme power, "the Royal Brute of Great Britain," who had caused all the trouble. It was therefore ridiculous for Americans to expect good King George to go out and slay the dragon for them. He himself was the dragon. America could set an example for the whole world by freeing itself from the rule of kings. "The cause of America is in great measure the cause of all mankind," he wrote. "'Tis not the concern of a day, a year, or an age; but of all ages to the end of time."

Common Sense was important because it brought the question of independence out into the open. It was also the first public attack

THOMAS PAINE

against the king. Tens of thousands of copies of the pamphlet were sold throughout the colonies, and its great success prompted other writers and political leaders to attack the king. They went too far. They blamed the king for everything. They pictured him as an evil man who could no longer fool them by hiding behind the skirts of his ministers. He was a monster, a "Royal criminal."

King George was, of course, neither an angel nor a devil. He was a rather average man, an extremely stubborn one, who firmly believed that no power on earth could stand against the might of the British Empire. His great pride had been wounded by the rough treatment of his troops at Lexington and Bunker Hill. Nothing could satisfy him now but a smashing victory that would bring the colonies to their knees.

England struck back at the colonies in a number of ways. She closed the New England fisheries, stopped all trade between the colonies and the mother country, withdrew her protection, and ordered her navy to capture all American ships at sea. These unfriendly acts proved to many Americans that the king was really as evil as *Common Sense* made him out to be.

HIRED SOLDIERS

In England there were many people who sympathized with the Americans. They believed Americans were fighting for the liberty of all

Englishmen. They were afraid that if the Americans were defeated, King George would gain in power even over his subjects at home, and the cause of liberty would suffer on both sides of the Atlantic. Most Englishmen agreed that it was probably necessary to crush the rebellion, but fighting Americans was something not many of them cared to do. A number of British officers resigned from the army rather than take part in the unpopular war.

The king's government found it so difficult to recruit men for the army in England that it hired professional soldiers from several small German states. Most of these soldiers came from a state called Hesse-Kassel, and came to be known in America as Hessians. The hiring of Hessians did more to arouse Americans and to destroy their faith in a saintly King George than had Paine's *Common Sense,* or anything England had done before. The colonists were shocked at the thought that King George would send hired butchers against his own subjects in America. One patriot wrote that any man who was foolish enough to still talk of making peace with the British "ought to be pelted with stones, by the children, when he walks the streets...."

Slowly, the American people were beginning to favor independence.

A Divided Country
1776

One chilly morning in April, General Howe stepped out of his Boston headquarters and stared in amazement at a hill called Dorchester Heights, to the south of the city. It had been fortified during the night by George Washington's rebel army. Strong breastworks of ice blocks and brown earth ran along the crest of the hill. Above the steepest slopes, barrels filled with rocks stood balanced, ready to be sent tumbling down the hill in the path of attacking troops.

Studying the hill through his glass, Howe could make out several companies of riflemen and some units with muskets. What disturbed him most were the cannon, all well placed on the top of the hill where they could pound Boston and a good part of the Royal Fleet in the harbor. None of the British cannon, from their low positions, could possibly place their shots farther than the bottom of the hill.

Howe made ready to attack, then changed his mind, probably haunted by the horrors of Bunker Hill. The British began making preparations to withdraw from the city. For the redcoats, the act of leaving Boston must have seemed like an escape from a prison city. They had been hemmed in there for many months, overcrowded, short of food and fuel. The civilian population had increased steadily, for a constant flow of colonial refugees had poured into the city to seek the protection of the British army. These refugees supported the mother country, and called themselves loyalists because of their loyalty to the king. During the winter they had caused serious food and housing problems, and greatly endangered the health of all.

WASHINGTON TAKES BOSTON

It may have been one of the loyalists who carried smallpox into the city. The disease had spread rapidly and raged for several weeks. Many had died. During that period Howe had lived in constant fear of rebel attack, for hundreds of his troops lay helpless in their beds.

Now that the British were about to leave Boston, the loyalists were frightened. Many were people of wealth whose property and homes had been taken from them by rebels. They had no place to go. Afraid of falling into the hands of the patriots, who regarded them as traitors, they begged General Howe not to leave them behind. Howe was a kindly man. He crowded them in with his troops and into every seagoing vessel he could find, and took them to Halifax, a port in Canada.

Wahington did not want to expose his troops to smallpox, and organized what was probably one of the most unusual military units of the war. It was a unit of troops with pock-marked faces, troops whose faces had been scarred by smallpox. Having once had the disease, they could be exposed to it again without danger. This unit of about 500 men was the first to enter Boston after the British had sailed away.

Fortunately for the Americans, the British had

CANNON FROM FORT TICONDEROGA WERE HAULED 300 MILES TO BOSTON.

been in such a hurry that they had left behind much of their military supplies, including ammunition, shot, small arms, and thousands of woolen blankets and shoes. Earlier, the Americans had captured the British supply ship *Nancy,* loaded with muskets, round shot, flints, and a brass mortar. All this, together with the cannon from the fallen British fort of Ticonderoga, provided Washington with enough military supplies to continue the war. But where would the British strike next? Washington thought they might try to take New York, the most important city in the colonies. To prevent that, he moved his army to New York and began throwing up breastworks to defend the city.

His success in driving the British out of Boston prompted many patriots to speak out boldly in favor of independence. In Philadelphia, Samuel Adams went before Congress and asked, "Why not declare for independence?" But others were more cautious. "Why all this haste?" asked a delegate from New York. Another said, "Before we are prepared to build a new house, why should we tear down the old one?"

The delegates knew that the people in their home colonies were sharply divided. In almost every American community there were patriots, who wanted independence; loyalists, who did not; and a group who did not take sides. It was not a struggle of poor against rich. People from all walks of life were to be found in each group.

THE LOYALISTS

The loyalists were a strange mixture of rich, poor, educated, and ignorant. Among them were people educated in England who felt more Brit-

A Divided Country

ish than American, people with strong family ties in England, colonial officials who had been appointed by the king and did not want to lose their jobs, and people who still believed in good King George. Some were loyalists simply because they wanted peace at any price. Among the loyalists, also, were well-informed persons who realized that the colonies were poorly prepared to fight the powerful British army, and timid ones who believed the colonies would be overrun by savage Indians and carved up by other European powers if they lost the protection of the mother country.

Included among the loyalists were settlers on the western frontiers of South Carolina and Georgia. They were in constant danger of Indian attack, and wanted the British army to protect them. Other frontiersmen suspected that the fight for independence had been planned by rich people on the eastern coast, who wanted to become rulers of a new American nation.

Among the rich loyalists were businessmen in large eastern cities who had become wealthy by trading with the British. They wanted to continue their profitable trade with the mother country, and were afraid that any change would destroy their businesses. They suspected that independence meant government by mob rule and violence, government under which the wealthy would enjoy no special advantages. They might even have their property taken from them and given to the poor.

THE PATRIOTS

Many owners of large plantations in the South were loyalists. They admired British manners and culture, and tried to create little worlds of British society on their plantations. They educated their sons in England, looked down on ordinary Americans, and believed that only people of education and wealth were fit to rule over others. They had always taken a leading part in colonial government, and believed their way of life could best be protected by remaining loyal to the king.

In Virginia, the oldest of the colonies, plantation owners felt a little closer to the American way of life. Some had been among the leaders in the fight against taxation without representation, but a good number of them were still undecided. Then Governor Dunmore did a number of things which helped them make up their minds. He secretly removed gunpowder stored in Williamsburg and loaded it aboard a British ship. The patriots armed themselves and surrounded the town to prevent the governor's escape. The governor was frightened. He made the mistake of offering to free all Negro slaves who came to his aid. There were rumors that he held secret meetings by night with Negro leaders, laying plans for a Negro uprising. There was also a rumor that the king himself was behind the planned uprising, and that any slave who killed his master would be rewarded with all the property his master had owned.

Panic swept through the colony, and the plantation owners no longer had any doubts about the need for independence. They became patriots. But since they still believed that only the upper classes were fit to rule, they looked forward to enjoying powerful positions in the new government.

Virginia became a patriot stronghold, as did New England. The small farmers and merchants of western Massachusetts felt even stronger about independence than did the hot-headed radicals of Boston. Many wealthy New Englanders who had won their fortunes through smuggling became leading patriots.

In the large port cities, where English influence on society and business had always been strong, the people of the upper classes usually remained loyal to the king. So many of New York's leading citizens sympathized with the British that it became fashionable for a time to be a loyalist. The Quakers and Germans in Pennsylvania refused to take sides. They were more interested in peace than in independence. In the Carolinas and Georgia, the feeling between patriots and loyalists had become so bitter that armed bands were organized to fight each other. The most important of their battles took place on February 27, 1776, at Moore's Creek Bridge. It ended in a victory for the patriots and gave them control of most of North Carolina.

Congress had no loyalist members by this time, but not all the delegates favored independence. Even radical Patrick Henry of Virginia felt it would be foolish to break away from England without first knowing what help might be expected from France and Spain. With the country divided against itself, there was little Congress could do except wait and hope for something to happen which might fan the flames of American liberty.

The Final Break

1776

The fog was lifting over New York early on the morning of June 29, 1776, when a man named Daniel McCurtin happened to glance out over the bay. At first he saw nothing but mist hanging low over the water, then suddenly he blinked and stared in amazement.

Later he tried to describe the scene. He wrote that he had "spied as I peeped out the Bay something resembling a wood of pine trees trimmed. I declare, at my noticing this, that I could not believe my eyes, but keeping my eyes fixed at the very spot, judge you of my surprise when in about ten minutes, the whole Bay was full of shipping as ever it could be. I declare that I thought all London was afloat."

Washington's lookouts on the shore of Long Island were blinking, too, as General Howe's mighty fleet of 130 ships arrived in the Lower Bay. This was the Army Howe had taken to Halifax after being forced out of Boston, but now it was greatly strengthened. The fleet anchored near Staten Island, shifting its anchorage in the bay several times during the next few days. The Americans waited, trying to guess where the attack would come. At Manhattan? Or Brooklyn? Or would Howe sail up the Hudson and attempt to join forces with a British army coming down from Canada by land?

Howe finally put his army ashore on Staten Island at the mouth of the harbor, which was not defended. The British were not yet ready to strike. They were awaiting reinforcements from England. The delay gave Washington more time to fortify his positions in Manhattan and across the East River on Brooklyn Heights. But to defend both places meant splitting his small army in half, with the East River between them. Had he kept all his forces in Manhattan, the British could have mounted cannon on Brooklyn Heights and destroyed the city.

New York was extremely difficult to defend. Yet, both Congress and Washington were anxious to prevent it from falling into British hands, for the loss of one of the most important cities in the colonies would frighten and discourage the colonial governments as well as the people. Many Americans, convinced that the war was a hopeless one, might then have joined the loyalists and forced the country to make peace with England.

The presence of thousands of American troops in New York did help the revolution in one way. It made the leading loyalists leave town, and gave the outspoken patriots in the army a chance to turn public opinion there in favor of independence. This kind of help was important, because it made the country more united. The patriots and committees helped, too, by writing pamphlets and articles about the need for independence. Thomas Paine said that America was the only stronghold of liberty left in the world. In Europe freedom lay crushed under the heels of kings and princes, and the same thing was about to happen in England. America must defend its freedom and "prepare in time an asylum for all mankind." Still another thing that helped independence was England's action in forcing American sailors to serve in the British navy. This was taken as proof that the English regarded the Americans as slaves.

One by one, the colonial governments instructed their delegates in Congress to vote for independence. Massachusetts, North Carolina, Georgia, and Virginia were the first to do so. By May, four colonies in New England and four in the South had declared in favor of independence. The middle colonies still remained undecided. They were not quite ripe, reported John Adams, "but they are very near it." Congress waited. The delay made the patriots impatient, and they blamed the delegates for being timid. One wrote

896

HOWE MOVED A FLEET OF 130 SHIPS INTO LOWER NEW YORK HARBOR.

to Samuel Adams, saying, "The people are ahead of you now." If Congress did not act quickly, soldiers and patriots would march on Philadelphia, get rid of Congress, and set up the kind of government that would carry out the will of the people.

THE DECLARATION

On June 7, Richard Henry Lee of Virginia asked Congress to decide "that these united colonies are, and ought to be, free and independent states . . ." After several days of debate, Lee said that there had already been too much talk. Why not vote now? "Let this happy day give birth to an American Republic! The eyes of Europe are fixed upon us. She demands of us a living example of freedom."

But the vote had to be held up for several weeks more, because some of the delegates were still awaiting instructions from home. Meanwhile, Congress chose a committee of five to write a Declaration of Independence—Thomas Jefferson, John Adams, Benjamin Franklin, Roger Sherman, and Robert Livingston. The committee turned over the actual work of writing the declaration to Thomas Jefferson, the tall gentleman farmer from Virginia, who they felt was the best writer among them. Jefferson was only thirty-three at the time, but his views were well known.

He believed it was better "to die free men rather than to live slaves." In one of his papers he had written that "God who gave us life, gave us liberty at the same time."

It took Jefferson eighteen days to write the Declaration of Independence. Later, he recalled that he had written it "without reference to book or pamphlet." He did not think it was his duty to "invent new ideas." The Declaration, he said, "was intended to be an expression of the American mind."

American ideas about government and politics were not new, nor were they invented by radical leaders to bring about revolution. The seeds of these ideas had come from such widely different things as religion, the "rights of Englishmen," life on the frontiers, and from a hundred and fifty years of colonial experience in self-government.

The Puritans who landed at Plymouth Rock, for example, brought with them the religious idea that all men are equal before God. This led them to the political idea that all men should be treated as equal by the law. In the minds of the colonists, America meant freedom. They had found freedom in the colonies because they lived so far away from the British king that he could no longer control their daily lives. But they had to pay for this new freedom by suffering the hardships of frontier life. They had to organize their own kind of society, set up local governments,

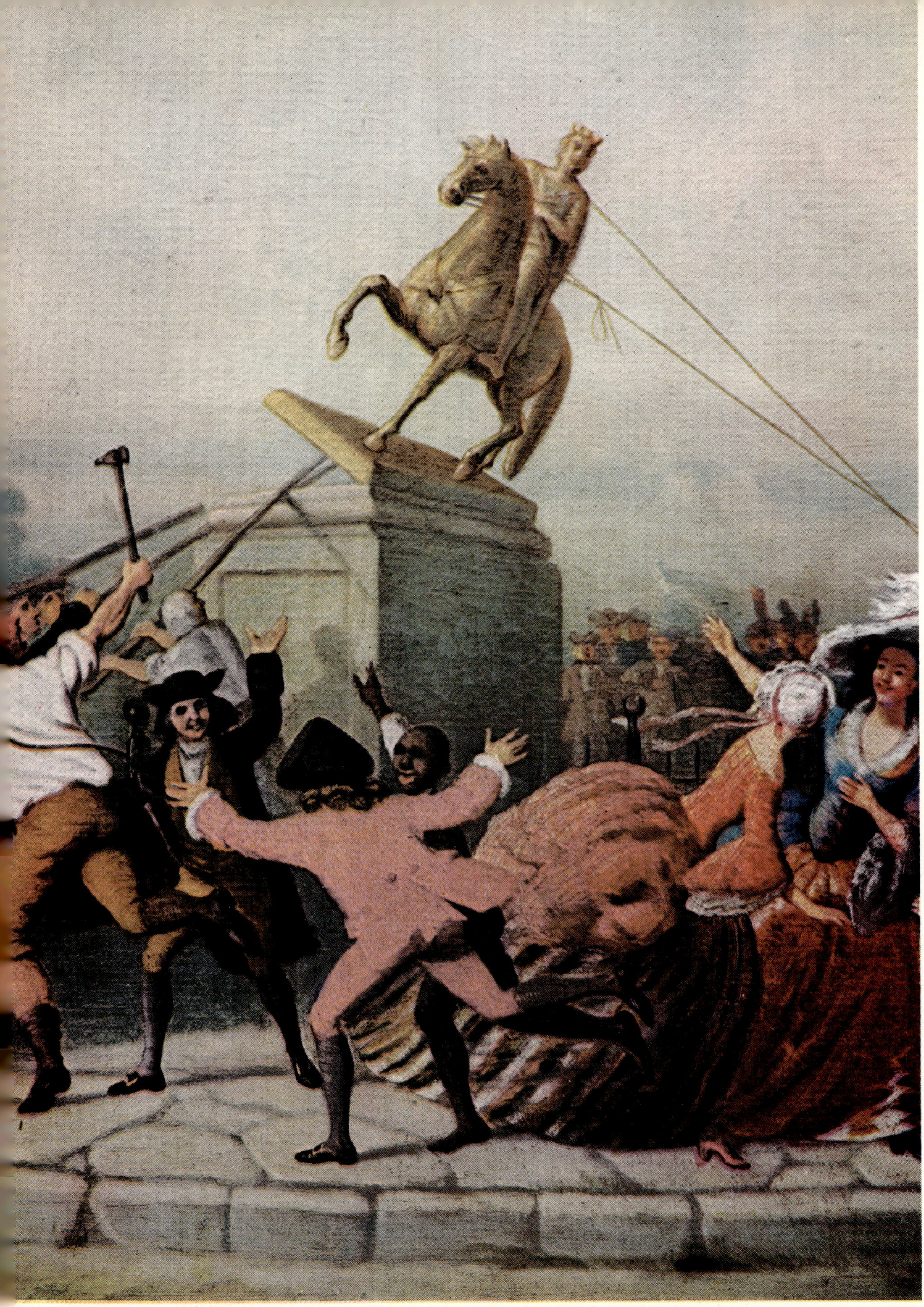

The Final Break

make their own laws, and settle their own community problems. They had learned how to care for themselves, and took pride in what they had accomplished. In time, they came to look upon freedom as something they had earned, something which now belonged to them, and which no one could take from them.

In England, where the rich owned the land, freedom of choice was limited for ordinary people. The only choice most of them had was whether to work for one rich person or another rich person. Their pay, in either case, would be very small. Freedom of choice in England, therefore, meant almost nothing, for it rarely gave anyone an opportunity to better himself. But in America, freedom of choice meant almost unlimited opportunity. Every man—except slaves—had a chance to better himself, and to use his ability in a way that would pay him well.

Thus freedom gave the colonies a new and richer way of life. It gave them confidence and dignity, and a feeling of independence. It led them to recognize the importance of the individual and his rights. It gave them a chance to discover that ordinary people could govern themselves.

Freedom was something the colonists lived and felt, but at first their lives were so active that they had little time to think about it. They never tried to put these feelings into words until England threatened their liberty. Then they struggled to explain their feelings. Colonial writers and speakers turned for help to an old book by John Locke, an Englishman. His book had nothing to do with America, but some of his political views were exactly like those held by the colonists and could be used to support the colonial cause.

Locke based his arguments on the natural rights of man, rights given by God to all men everywhere. He wrote that the power to govern came from the people. They gave that power to the government. Therefore it was the government's duty to serve the people and to act for the good of all. If it failed to do so, the people could do away with it and set up another government that would serve them better.

Locke's ideas were very popular among the colonists in 1776. Jefferson knew this. He also understood the wordless feelings the colonists had about freedom and life and government. These were the things he tried to put into words so that the Declaration of Independence would be an "expression of the American mind." At the beginning of the Declaration, Jefferson listed some great truths that applied to all men everywhere. This listing was important because the Declaration was written for the peoples of all the world, so that they would understand, approve and be inspired by the American Revolution.

JULY 4, 1776

The first of the great truths listed is "That all men are created equal . . ." They are equal before God and equal before the law. Jefferson and the other delegates knew that the slaves were not treated as equals, but the fact that some men were being denied equality did not change the great truth. Congress was saying, in effect, that all men had the right to be recognized and treated as equals. Congress was setting up a goal, pointing the way toward a more perfect form of society.

Another of the great truths set forth is that God gave all men certain rights which cannot be taken from them; and that among these rights are life, liberty, and the chance to search for happiness.

The Declaration states that people organize governments to protect these rights, and that such governments receive their power from the people themselves. Whenever a government fails to protect these rights the people can make changes in the government, or do away with it, and set up some other form of government to provide for their safety and happiness.

The Declaration then continues with a long list of complaints against the king, showing how his government failed to protect the rights of the American people. The list was intended to prove that King George III "is unfit to be the ruler of a free people."

On July 2, Congress voted for a separation from England. It then considered the Declaration of Independence, and passed it on July 4, 1776.

Now at last Americans knew exactly what they were fighting for: independence, the natural rights of man, and the kind of self-government under which all men could be free and equal.

IN 1776, A CROWD OF NEW YORKERS PULLED DOWN THE STATUE OF KING GEORGE III.

The Old Fox
1776-1777

The cold winter winds howled through the streets of New York, but the houses were filled with warmth and good cheer, and the merry crackle of hearth fires. It was late in December of 1776. Six months earlier the city had been the headquarters of General Washington's ragged army of patriots. Now it was in the hands of the British, and they were in a mood to celebrate.

Some redcoats were making ready for Christmas. Others were writing long letters home to England, saying that the war was almost over. They told how Washington had been driven out of New York, how the British had stormed Fort Washington just north of the city and captured 2,600 American troops and large stores of military supplies. They told how Washington's army had crossed the Hudson River, and how General Cornwallis, with a large force of redcoats and Hessians, had chased him across the state of New Jersey.

At his headquarters in New York, General Howe was preparing to spend a pleasant winter among his loyalist friends. He had many reasons for being cheerful. On December 13th, he had captured General Charles Lee, second in command of the American forces under Washington. The British had met with little resistance as they chased Washington through New Jersey, and now some British units were as deep into New Jersey as Bordentown, only twenty-five miles from Philadelphia. Howe was particularly pleased by the fact that thousands of colonists in New Jersey had welcomed the British, and had taken advantage of his offer to pardon all who renewed their oaths of allegiance to King George.

What was left of Washington's army had escaped across the Delaware River into Pennsylvania. Howe knew that most of the troops under Washington would be free to go home after their term of enlistment ran out at the end of the year. This would leave Washington with almost no army at all, and Howe was convinced that the rebellion was almost over. He ordered his troops to find winter quarters for themselves in various towns of New Jersey. He also gave General Cornwallis leave to return to England for a few months of vacation.

In Pennsylvania, camped in the frozen hills not far from the Delaware River, Washington was preparing for action. In the last twelve weeks he had suffered one defeat after another, lost five thousand of his best troops, most of his cannon, and large stores of ammunition. Unless he acted quickly, most of his troops would be returning to their homes, for their enlistments came to an end on December 31st. After that date the American army would be reduced to about 1,400 troops.

CROSSING THE DELAWARE

The Americans broke camp late in the afternoon of Christmas Day, for a surprise attack on the Hessians at Trenton. They reached the Delaware river just before nightfall, then began the slow work of crossing the ice-choked river to the New Jersey side under cover of darkness. There were not nearly enough boats. Many trips had to be made back and forth, and horses and cannon had to be ferried across on clumsy barges. Sleet began to fall an hour before midnight, and with it came strong gusts of wind that threatened to upset the troops' overloaded boats. In the darkness it was impossible to avoid the floating cakes of ice. They thumped against the bows and frail sides of the boats, showering the men with icy spray. The crossing was completed just as the first streaks of dawn brightened the eastern sky.

Washington sent some of his troops under General Sullivan along the river road, while he and General Nathanael Greene and their divisions followed the Pennington Road, approaching the town of Trenton from the north. Washington knew the success of his attack depended upon complete surprise. If the Hessians were prepared, they could easily hold the town for several hours. That would be long enough to bring up Hessians from other towns, and Washington's army would then find itself trapped on the New Jersey side of the river.

The Hessians in Trenton had celebrated Christmas in the hearty German fashion, with much eating and drinking, just as Washington had hoped. Their commander, Colonel Rall, and most of his troops were still in bed when the Americans struck at Trenton from two sides. At the sound of gunfire the Hessians leaped out of bed, dressed, snatched up their weapons, and stumbled out to defend the town. They were still struggling to get into their coats as they fell into formation. They tried to advance northward on the two main streets, but were scattered by screaming round shot from American cannon.

Then Colonel Rall mounted his horse and led an advance up Broad Street, but now the Americans had come up between the houses and were firing from both sides of the street. At the same time General Sullivan's American troops swept in between the Hessians, making retreat impossible. The one-sided battle soon came to an end. The Hessians lost 970 men, including 920 prisoners. Four Americans were wounded.

News of the American victory stunned General Howe in New York. He canceled General Cornwallis' trip to England, and sent him to take command of the troops in New Jersey. Cornwallis moved swiftly. He arrived at Princeton on January 1, 1777, and marched toward Trenton the following day. He reached Washington's main line of defense along the south bank of the Assunpink Creek just before dark. Cornwallis decided to hold up his attack on the American position until the following morning. As he saw

WASHINGTON CROSSED THE DELAWARE AND ATTACKED TRENTON, TAKING THE HESSIANS COMPLETELY BY SURPRISE.

it, there was no great need to hurry, since the Americans were hopelessly trapped, with their backs to the Delaware River.

Washington and his officers knew that they could not defend their position along the creek. The Americans were greatly outnumbered, and any attempt to retreat across the river in the few boats available would have resulted in the capture of most of their troops. But there was one thing they could do. They could slip around the right side of the British forces during the night, strike at Princeton in the morning, and then go on to attack the main British supply base at New Brunswick.

THE BATTLE OF PRINCETON

To fool the British, Washington left a detail of four hundred men behind to dig trenches, make all the usual camp noises, and keep the campfires burning brightly. These men were ordered to follow the main army just before dawn. Washington's troops slipped silently out of camp before midnight, with the wheels of their gun carriages wrapped in rags to keep them from making any noise on the frozen roads that might alert the British.

When Cornwallis awoke the following morning, he was puzzled by the silence in the American encampment. There seemed to be no sign of life at all. Moments later he heard a dull rumble in the north. Could it be thunder? The rumbling came again. This time he recognized it as the booming of cannon. The "old fox" had fooled him again.

To the north, at Stony Bridge near Princeton, two British regiments had suddenly come face to face with a column of Americans under General Mercer. In the fight that followed, Mercer was killed. Some of the British retreated to Princeton, and were soon routed by Washington's main army. In these two small battles each side lost about one hundred men in dead and wounded, and the Americans captured nearly three hundred prisoners.

Washington now realized that his hope of going on to strike at the British supply base in

WASHINGTON OUTFOXED THE BRITISH AND WON THE BATTLE OF PRINCETON.

New Brunswick was out of the question. His men were too tired and hungry. They had gone without sleep for some forty hours. He gave them a hearty meal from British supplies, and a short rest.

The British army reached Princeton just after the Americans had left, but Cornwallis gave up the chase and continued on to Brunswick to protect the main base. Washington headed for a high ridge of hills at Morristown. There he could defend himself against a stronger force, and yet be in a position to threaten any move the British might make up the Hudson or into New Jersey.

The victories at Trenton and Princeton gave Americans new hope. They hailed Washington as a military genius. Patriots in New Jersey felt so certain of victory that they formed armed bands and attacked British outposts and wagon trains, forcing most of the redcoats and Hessians to concentrate in areas close to New York city. In Paris, news of the victories made it easier for Benjamin Franklin to obtain more loans, guns, and ammunition from the French. But Washington lost most of his experienced soldiers shortly after their enlistments ran out, and he was faced with the slow and difficult task of building his army all over again. Fortunately, his victories marked the end of fighting for a number of months.

Long delays between battles were common during the war. The slow pace made it possible for Washington to rebuild his army time and again, for his troops deserted him by the thousands every winter. One of Washington's disadvantages was that he did not have the support of a real government. The United States of America was nothing more than a shadowy association of free states. Congress had very limited powers. It could not tax the people. It had to beg the states for money in order to carry on the war. The states did as they pleased about these requests, and usually paid only a small portion of what they were asked to give.

Some states were actually afraid of building up a strong American army. Such an army, they feared, might be tempted to set up a powerful military government that would have the states at its mercy. To protect themselves, the states organized small armies of militiamen over which they had complete control. Some of these units were loaned to Washington at times, but they were usually not very effective. As a result, Washington was never able to raise a large enough army to drive the British from American soil. Poor roads and long supply lines also slowed down the pace of the war. Washington spent many months waiting for military supplies from France. These had to be slipped into the country through the British naval blockade, and some of them failed to get through.

THE STRENGTH OF AMERICA

But the Americans also had certain advantages. They were on their native soil. They knew how to live off the land, and how to fight in the wilderness. They could travel lighter and faster than could the British, who were usually slowed down by heavy guns and long wagon trains. Furthermore, they did not need to defeat the British. As long as they could keep an army in the field, the war would go on. The British, on the other hand, could not bring the rebellion to an end without defeating the Americans.

The Americans also had the great advantage of having George Washington as their military leader. True, his war experience was limited; he made a number of mistakes, and was defeated in battle many times. Yet, even when everything went wrong and the American cause seemed all but lost, he never gave up hope. His patience seemed endless. He knew how to wait for just the right moment to strike, and how to win the battles that counted most. It was Washington's fighting spirit and rocklike character, more than anything else, that kept the revolution alive.

As for the British, they had large, well-supplied armies with trained soldiers and experienced officers. Their navy controlled the sea and blockaded the Atlantic ports. They could move their armies on ships and strike swiftly at any point along the coast. Loyalists acted as spies and kept them informed of American movements. Thousands of loyalists joined the British army and fought against their own countrymen. But the British were three thousand miles away from home, and supplies and troops were slow in coming. Furthermore, British officers had been trained in the European style of warfare. In Europe, a war could be won by capturing the large manufacturing centers, thus cutting the enemy off from its source of supply. In America, there were no large manufacturing centers. The strength of America lay in thousands of small farms and towns. An American army could be defeated at one point, only to re-form and carry on the war again a hundred miles away. General Howe, the British commander, seemed to be in no hurry to end the war. He took his time between campaigns, believing that the Americans would soon become discouraged and lay down their arms. That was what he wanted—peace, on British terms, with as little bloodshed as possible. Then the War Office in London drew up a plan to cut the troublesome New England states off from the rest of the country. To accomplish this, General John Burgoyne was to lead an army southward from Canada to Albany. General Howe in New York was to lead his army up the Hudson and join Burgoyne at Albany. Burgoyne received his orders and began moving southward in June of 1777, but, through some mistake in London, General Howe never did receive his instructions to move up the Hudson.

The Road to Yorktown
1777-1781

The big English setter did not look like a stray dog. When it came wandering into Washington's camp one day in the fall of 1777, a soldier brought it to his officer. The officer took it directly to Washington's headquarters and pointed out the name on the dog's collar—"General Howe." Washington had the dog fed while he wrote a polite note to General Howe. Half an hour later, the dog and the note were sent to the British camp under a flag of truce.

The incident was not important, but it gave the Americans something to laugh and joke about for several days. There had not been much cause for laughter in recent weeks. General Howe had taken Philadelphia, America's capital and its largest city, after defeating Washington at Brandywine and at Germantown. Washington's losses had been heavy. He was now camped in the hills of Valley Forge, some twenty miles from Philadelphia, in desperate need of supplies of all kinds.

In the North, moving down from Montreal, General Burgoyne had captured the fort at Ticonderoga, and had continued on to Fort Edwards on the Hudson. Burgoyne, however, was having his troubles, too. He was almost out of food, and his supply base at Montreal lay 185 miles north, through almost trackless wilderness.

Burgoyne knew that east of him there were large stores of food and many cattle at Bennington, in what is now Vermont. He sent out a detachment of 1,300 men to raid the place and to bring back all the cattle and horses they could find. The detachment marched into a trap which had been set for it by John Stark and his New England militia, and when the short battle was over, the British had lost. American losses were thirty killed and forty wounded. The Indians with Burgoyne lost faith in his leadership and deserted him. He now had no choice but to wait in the wilderness for supplies from Montreal, and that meant a delay of at least a month.

The delay gave an American army under General Gates time to establish itself in the upper valley of the Hudson. Gates' army grew rapidly as he waited, for the American victory at Bennington prompted thousands of patriots to join his forces. When the British and Americans finally met at Freeman's farm, the British were driven back. They retreated toward Saratoga, but Burgoyne soon found himself surrounded by Americans. On October 17, 1777, he surrendered, giving up his ivory-hilted sword to Gates.

FRANCE ENTERS THE WAR

Burgoyne's defeat at Saratoga was the turning point of the war. Some five thousand redcoats, nearly a fourth of the British troops in America, were taken prisoner. News of the American victory was enough to bring France into the war on the side of the Americans, and, later, Spain and Holland also declared war on England. The kings of these three countries did not join the fight in order to support the American rebellion. In fact, they were uneasy about it. They did not believe in freedom for the individual, and were very much against the idea that the common man was fit to govern himself. But all of them hated and feared England, and they felt that their best chance to defeat her was to strike while she was having difficulties with her American colonies.

France sent her navy to threaten the British supply lines across the Atlantic. She also loaned the Americans money, and sent large shipments of clothing, war supplies, and food. Many months were to pass, however, before any of these supplies reached General Washington. Meanwhile, shortages of food, clothing, and shoes caused extreme hardship at Valley Forge that winter. Almost 4,000 troops were reported unfit for duty, and 3,000 deserted. Washington begged Congress for help. "Few men have more than one shirt and some none at all," he wrote. "Men in camp are unfit for duty because they are barefoot and otherwise naked. For want of blankets, numbers are obliged to sit up all night by the fires instead of taking comfortable rest in a natural way."

It was at Valley Forge that two outstanding foreigners joined Washington's army. One was a young nobleman from France, the Marquis de Lafayette. He became a close friend of Washington, and used his influence to get more active support from the French. The other was a German military man, Baron von Steuben. He trained Washington's troops and young officers, and built the American army into a more effective fighting machine than it had ever been before.

In Philadelphia, General Henry Clinton replaced Howe as commander of the British forces in America. He gave up Philadelphia, marched his army back to New York, and soon launched a new campaign in the southern states. There were many loyalists in the South, and he counted upon their strong support. General Clinton believed he could win the war by taking possession of the country, section by section, starting in the South and working north.

The southern campaign began with the capture of Savannah, Georgia, in December, 1778. By the following summer the British were occupying large areas in Georgia and South Carolina. They cornered an American army under General Benjamin Lincoln at Charleston, and forced him to surrender his army and the city in May of 1780. Five thousand American troops were taken prisoner, in the most serious American defeat of the war. Three months later the Americans lost another battle and two thousand troops when Cornwallis defeated General Gates at Camden.

During all this time, Washington's army remained near the Hudson to serve as a constant threat against Clinton's army in New York. Lafayette had been in Paris for over a year. He returned to Washington's camp with wonderful news. He had persuaded the French to send 6,000 of their best troops to America under the command of General Rochambeau, and they were already at sea.

A TRAP FOR CORNWALLIS

Washington placed General Nathanael Greene in charge of the American forces in the South. Greene lost a number of battles, but he slowly wore out the enemy with his long marches and surprise attacks. For Clinton's plan for conquering the South by sections had one great weakness: he did not have enough troops to defend the areas he had already won. Most of his regulars were needed as combat troops by Cornwallis, who commanded British forces in the South. Cornwallis failed to get as much support from southern loyalists as he had expected, and those who joined his army could rarely be depended

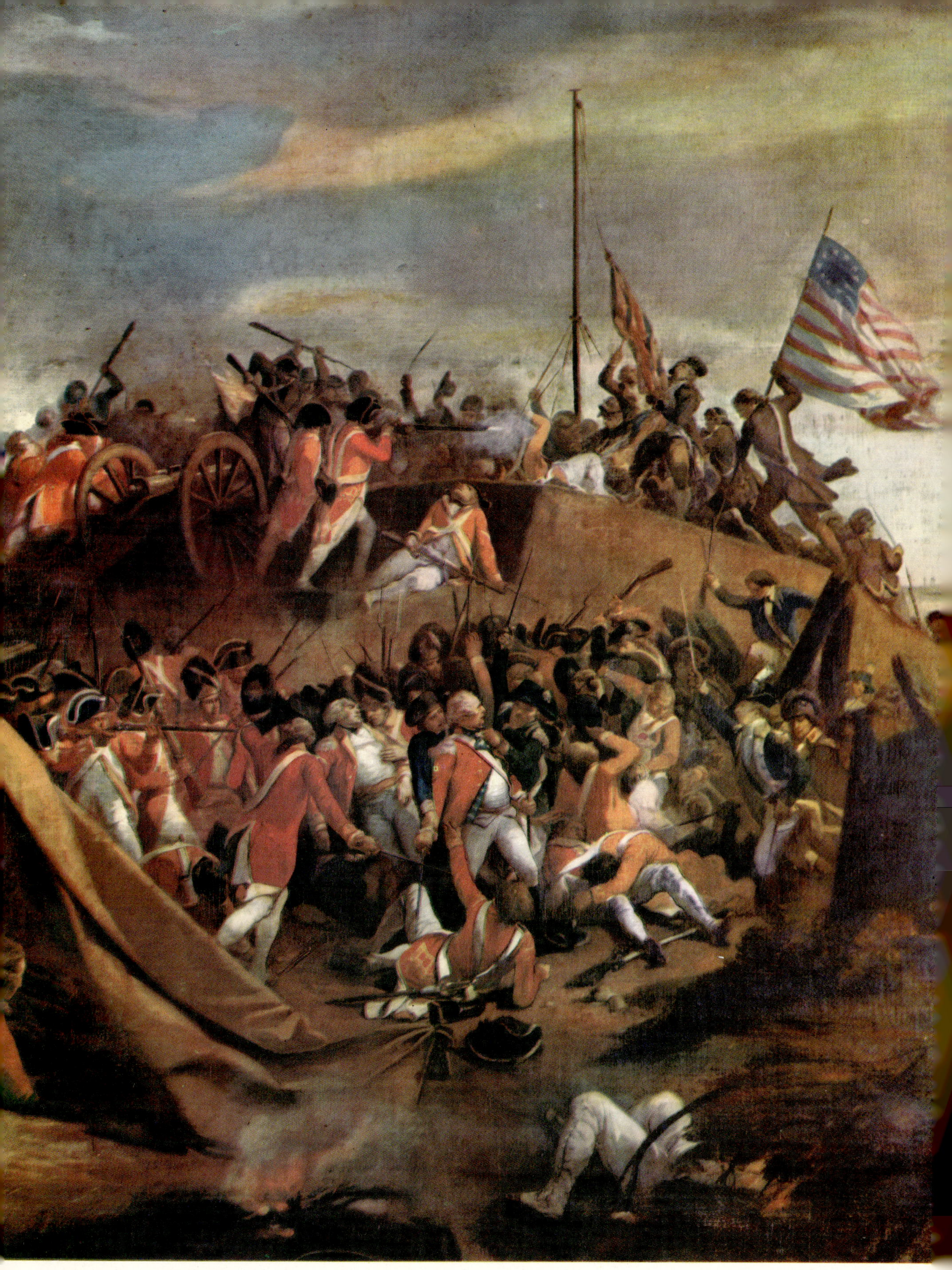

The Road to Yorktown

AMERICAN AND FRENCH TROOPS STORMED THE BRITISH DEFENSES AT YORKTOWN.

upon when they were most needed. The British did leave small units of regulars and loyalists behind to guard various strong points they had taken. But Greene, with the help of armed bands of patriots, struck at these strong points and forced the British to withdraw from a number of them.

By this time, Cornwallis had lost faith in the southern loyalists and in Clinton's plan for taking the South. Having failed to destroy Greene's army, Cornwallis marched northward into Virginia. There, for a time, he carried on a cat-and-mouse campaign against a small American army under Lafayette, trying to force the Americans into battle. When this attempt failed, Cornwallis withdrew to Yorktown on the coast, at the mouth of Chesapeake Bay, and began to fortify it.

In the middle states, Washington was still a threat to Clinton's army in New York, but three years of waiting for action had made Washington's troops restless. Keeping trained regulars in the army had become more difficult than ever, for Congress was paying the soldiers with paper money that was almost worthless. Washington complained, "A wagon-load of money will scarcely buy a wagon-load of provisions."

Washington was also unhappy about the French army commanded by General Rochambeau. It had landed at Newport, Rhode Island, a year ago, and had been there waiting ever since. The French had refused to join in an attack on New York. The city was too well fortified to be taken by land forces alone, Rochambeau believed. Washington had finally written to Admiral de Grasse, commander of a large French fleet then in the West Indies, explaining the problem, and asking him to come north and help attack New York.

On August 14, 1781, Washington received his answer. De Grasse regretted he could not go north as far as New York; he had to return to the West Indies in the fall. But he was sailing his fleet north to Chesapeake Bay in the hope that he might be useful there. He was bringing with him 3,000 troops and some cannon.

At once Washington changed his plans. Yorktown was located on a narrow strip of land with wide rivers on each side and the ocean at one end. With the French fleet in Chesapeake Bay, he could close in on Cornwallis from land and sea. Lafayette and his small American army were already in the area.

To keep the British in New York guessing, Washington ordered his men to begin building fortifications on the New Jersey side of the Hudson River, just opposite New York. He also spread the rumor that a big attack on New York was about to be launched. One morning late in August, General Clinton learned from his spies that the Americans were gone. Their large encampment across the river was vacant. Later, he learned that Washington's army and the French army of Rochambeau were marching southward through New Jersey.

Cornwallis, meanwhile, was still building his fortifications at Yorktown. He had so much faith in the British navy that he did not regard the Yorktown peninsula as a dangerous trap. The ocean at his back was like a friendly doorway through which he could receive aid and supplies from the British fleet. If he were to be attacked by a large enemy force, his fortifications could hold out long enough for him to get reinforcements by sea. If the enemy became too strong, he could ask the navy to take him off the peninsula, thus allowing him to strike at some other place along the coast.

THE BATTLE OF YORKTOWN

Washington, too, had respect for the British navy. He did not know where it was, but he realized that it could prevent him from gaining a victory over Cornwallis. Then, shortly after the Americans had passed through Philadelphia on the long march to Virginia, a rider came galloping up from the South with a letter from Admiral de Grasse. The French fleet had arrived at Chesapeake Bay, landing 3,000 troops on James Island. Washington was so filled with joy that for once he forgot his dignity. He became so excited that he ran to Rochambeau, waving his hat in the air as he shouted the wonderful news.

Victory seemed certain—provided the British navy did not arrive to upset his plans. Now speed was important; every day was precious. The two armies quickened their pace. They marched through Baltimore, and a day later they crossed the Potomac River and entered Virginia. When they reached Williamsburg, Washington was again greeted with cheerful news. Admiral

THE SURRENDER OF CORNWALLIS AT YORKTOWN MARKED THE REAL END OF THE WAR.

de Grasse had spotted the British fleet at sea, had sailed out to meet it, and had defeated it in battle. The French fleet was now in complete control of the sea. Cornwallis was hopelessly surrounded.

Washington brought up his cannon and began the mightiest artillery attack of the war. The big guns boomed day after day. Cornwallis was forced to withdraw from his outer defenses. The French and Americans moved in closer and hammered away at Yorktown itself with two hundred cannon. By October 14, they were storming the British redoubts, and a counterattack two days later failed to push them back.

Finally, at ten o'clock on Wednesday morning, October 17, a drummer boy in a red coat climbed to the top of a British breastwork and began beating his drum. But the sound of his drumming could not be heard above the constant thunder of cannon fire, and clouds of swirling smoke made him almost impossible to see. Then, in a moment when the smoke cleared a little, someone spotted him.

Orders were passed to the gunners, and the big guns stopped firing. A British officer appeared on the breastwork beside the drummer and waved a white handkerchief. As he came forward, an American officer ran out to meet him, blindfolded him, and led him back behind the lines. The Englishman carried a letter from Cornwallis asking for a twenty-four-hour truce to arrange for the terms of surrender. Slowly the dust and smoke of battle drifted away, revealing the clear blue of the autumn sky. The American and French soldiers, a little timid at first, came out of their trenches and looked around, as if puzzled by the uneasy stillness. Before long, many of them stretched out on the ground and fell fast asleep in full view of the British.

A WORLD TURNED UPSIDE DOWN

On the afternoon of October 19, 1781, the French and American armies marched out in a field beyond Yorktown and formed two long

FRENCH AND AMERICANS LINED UP TO WATCH THE BRITISH GIVE UP THEIR ARMS.

lines facing each other. A column of British soldiers, 7,000 in all, filed slowly out of Yorktown and passed between the two lines, their drums and fifes playing an English tune called "The World Turned Upside Down." At the end of the field the British stacked their guns, laid down their drums and colors, and returned to Yorktown to await further orders as prisoners of war.

With the surrender of Cornwallis at Yorktown, the war all but came to an end. For a time Greene continued his campaign in the South. Late in 1782, the British withdrew from Charleston and Savannah, and held only one city in the entire country—New York. Peace came at last with the signing of the Treaty of Paris on January 20, 1783. England recognized the independence of the United States of America, giving the new nation all territory north to Canada, west to the Mississippi, and south to Florida.

The American victory over the strongest colonial power in the world prompted other colonies to think about independence, too. In South America, for example, local leaders tried to stir up the people by pointing out the unfair way they were being treated by their Spanish rulers. The American Revolution also influenced the people of Europe. They had watched it from beginning to end, feeling that it was not so much a war for independence as it was a revolt of a people against their king. They themselves had lived and suffered under royal rulers for many centuries, and to them the war meant a fight for the rights and freedom of ordinary people, and the success of the revolution, a great victory for the common man.

The United States joined the family of nations as an equal, and began a bold experiment with a new form of government, a republic, one in which the people ruled over themselves through their chosen representatives. Whether a republic could succeed or not was a question no one could answer. But the fact that the American people had been able to set up their own form of government gave ordinary people the world over new hope, and planted the seeds of rebellion in many lands.

THE FRENCH REVOLUTION

Champion of Liberty
1782-1789

WHEN THE MARQUIS DE LAFAYETTE returned to France in 1782, after taking part in the American Revolution, he was hailed as a popular hero. It was pleasant to be welcomed as a champion of liberty. But he had been in America so long that he was beginning to see his own country as an American might see it, and he was troubled. France was one of the largest and richest countries in Europe, and yet the wealth of the nation was in the hands of a few, while the great majority of the people had almost nothing. He found a disturbing emptiness in the faces of the people. On country roads, peasants often stared at him with hollow eyes and blank faces. They seemed to have so little to live for. The nobles and the rich had discovered ways of avoiding taxes, and the entire tax burden fell on the poor,

THE MARQUIS DE LAFAYETTE

who scarcely had enough for themselves and their families.

These were the people who now turned to Lafayette, hoping that he might lead them in their fight for liberty. Lafayette was eager to help them. "When one loves liberty," he explained, "one is not at peace until after having established it in one's own country." He and thousands of other Frenchmen believed the people of France could win liberty for themselves if they followed the example set for them by the Americans. Many had read Thomas Paine's famous pamphlet *Common Sense,* which had stirred the Americans in their fight for liberty. Many had also studied the rights of man listed in the Declaration of Independence. Writers pointed out in newspapers and books that these rights belonged to all men everywhere, and that they had always been denied to ordinary Frenchmen. The French had been cheered by the American victory, and hoped that they, too, could somehow win liberty for themselves. But there were great differences between the two countries—differences which made it impossible for the American Revolution to to serve as an exact model for France.

The American ideas about liberty had been developed and tested by the colonists for a hundred and fifty years before the revolt against England. During that time they had established a free society and had learned how to govern themselves through elected representatives. To them, liberty was as real as sunshine and rain. The American Revolution, therefore, was a fight to protect a way of life which the British king was threatening to destroy.

Liberty in France, on the other hand, was little more than a hope. It was something people read about and talked about and wanted to experience. Power had always been in the hands of kings and nobles. The ordinary people of France, some ninety-six per cent of the total population, had no voice in the government. And so, before there could be liberty in France, there would have to be sweeping changes in government and society. The French would have to wipe out class differences, uprooting a way of life which had been in existence for many centuries. Yet, the liberal leaders of France seemed to believe that all this could be accomplished in an orderly manner without bloodshed. Most of these leaders were against violence. They knew, of course, that no important changes could be brought about peacefully without the consent of the king. But they felt he would not stand in the way of these changes for long because the public demands for them were becoming louder and louder.

THE RIGHTS OF MAN

It was not necessary for the liberal leaders to point out the evils of the French system of government. That had been done time and again, over a period of at least sixty years, by Voltaire, Montesquieu, Rousseau, and other famous writers. These men had led the French out of the age of ignorance and superstition into a new age of reason where people were better informed and dared to think for themselves.

Although these writers had not agreed on many things, most of them admired the British system of government, its law-making Parliament, its fine courts, its freedom of press and religion, and held them up as examples for the French to follow. They had led the fight against the torture of prisoners, cruel punishments, and the practice of treating all suspects as guilty until proven innocent. In general, they had encouraged people to think for themselves and to speak out against wrongful uses of power by the church and by the government.

Rousseau had been a champion of the rights of man. He agreed with the English writer John Locke that all people had the right to life, liberty, and property. It was the duty of government, he said, to protect these natural rights of its citizens. He also believed that the government received its authority to govern from the consent of the people. Such ideas were well known and widely accepted in France long before the American Revolution. The American victory was taken as proof that these ideas were not only right, but practical as well, and made the people more impatient than ever in their demands for better government. They were willing to follow anyone who would lead them to freedom.

LAFAYETTE AND FREEDOM

And yet there was little that Lafayette could do. He did use his influence to promote religious freedom, so that Protestants in France would no longer be treated unfairly. He also worked to outlaw the slave trade. He suggested that the king free his slaves in Guiana, a French possession in South America. Each of the newly freed slaves, he said, should be given a piece of land upon which he could earn his living. When the government showed no interest in his plan, Lafayette bought two plantations and forty-eight Negro slaves in Guiana. He arranged to give the slaves special training, intending to release them as soon as they could care for themselves. When he wrote George Washington about the plan, Washington replied it was striking proof "of the goodness of your heart . . . God grant that a like spirit may come to . . . all the people of this country!"

In 1784, Lafayette visited America, where he asked Washington's advice on how to gain freedom for the French. Washington was unable to help him. He pointed out that the Americans were still trying to establish a representative form of government under which they could enjoy the freedom they had won. The states had still to form a union and write a constitution. On the subject of slavery, Washington said that he and Jefferson would support any plan that would free all the slaves in Virginia. But there was danger in such a plan, he said, because many white people still refused to open their eyes to the truth that all Americans, regardless of color, had the right to enjoy liberty and equality as citizens. At the same time, Washington encouraged Lafayette to go on with his plan of freeing his slaves in French Guiana, and gave him a large sum of money to help pay expenses.

LAFAYETTE ASKED WASHINGTON FOR ADVICE ON GOVERNING A REPUBLIC.

KING LOUIS' LAVISH COURT ADDED TO THE GOVERNMENT'S DEBTS.

Returning to France, Lafayette felt like a man with his hands tied. There were so many things that needed doing, and so little that he could do by himself. He became restless. He often visited the new American ambassador, Thomas Jefferson, and there he met other Frenchmen who thought as he did. They spent many hours together discussing the problems of France. The king, Louis XVI, meant well, but he was a weak man with little interest in the affairs of government. He was too easily influenced by his extravagant wife, the unpopular Marie Antoinette, and others, and surrounded himself with weak ministers. Most of the ministers remained in office only a few months, and seemed more interested in retirement pensions for themselves than in government business.

Another problem that deeply troubled Lafayette—and all Frenchmen—was that of money. France was deeply in debt, partly because of the American Revolution. The government had borrowed such huge sums to aid the Americans that

914

most of the taxes it collected had to be used just to pay interest on the loans. Each year the government was forced to borrow still more money to pay for the expenses of running the country. Now the national treasury was empty, and it was almost impossible for France to get more loans.

Taxes had already been raised so high that it was impossible to raise them again. Furthermore, the taxes came from the people who could least afford it—the lower and middle classes. The nobles and the Church were required to pay very little, and rich businessmen could avoid paying in dishonest ways.

Because of the money problem, something happened that allowed Lafayette to take action at last. Calonne, the king's minister of the treasury, called an Assembly of Notables together to consider the tax question and other government problems. He chose the members of the assembly himself, and among them was Lafayette. All the members were noblemen, but they represented the various regions of France, and the Church as well.

When the Assembly of Notables met in February of 1787, Calonne presented an outline of his program. Although the assembly had no power to make laws, it could make recommendations to the king. Calonne hoped the approval of his program would influence the king to carry it out. He asked the assembly members to recommend changes in the law that would greatly increase their taxes and cut down on their privileges as noblemen. Most of them opposed it. Lafayette and other liberals opposed it for different reasons. They felt it did not go far enough.

Instead of discussing Calonne's program, the members used the opportunity to find fault with him as a minister. Lafayette asked the assembly to recommend full rights of citizenship for Protestants, which it did. Later he spoke out against dishonesty in government, and asked the king to call a meeting of an elected body of representatives from all classes, known as the Estates General. The members of the assembly were shocked at Lafayette's boldness. The Estates General was something from the past; it had not been in existence for 175 years. Did Lafayette realize what he was saying? Why, it was like telling the king that the nobles no longer had confidence in him, that they wanted him to turn his law-making powers over to the representatives of the people.

While the assembly refused to act on Lafayette's suggestion, the idea was immediately picked up by writers in newspapers and pamphlets. Everywhere in France, people began to demand that an Estates General be called to bring about the changes that France needed. Even the members of the assembly began to change their minds. Lafayette was delighted with the public's support of his views. He mentioned it in a letter to Washington, saying that "the King and family . . . don't forgive me for the liberties I have taken, and the success it had among the other classes of people."

THE KING TAXES THE NOBLES

Calonne became so unpopular with the assembly that the king dismissed him and appointed Brienne in his place. The new minister tried to work out a program which would please the nobles, but they refused to approve his tax plan. They said that, in fact, they had no authority to approve taxes, and hinted that only the Estates General had the power to do so. The king dismissed the Assembly of Notables in May of 1787, and made new laws providing for certain changes and new taxes. These laws were sent to be registered by the high courts of appeal in the various provinces. All the king's laws or decrees had to be registered in this way, so that the courts of the land would have a record of them and could enforce them. The high courts of appeal could make comments about the new laws; the king could act on them or not as he pleased.

Over the course of the years, these courts had tried to strengthen themselves by declaring that they were one body, representing all the people of France, and that one of their duties was to protect the people from bad laws made by the king. When the king sent them a law they did not like, they simply refused to register it. But these courts did not in fact represent the people. The judges were all nobles. They owned their judgeships, and passed them down from father to son. Naturally, they were against any laws which would take power away from the courts, or would weaken the special privileges of the nobility. They were also very much against any laws that made the nobles pay their share of the taxes.

King Louis XVI's new laws did indeed place a heavy tax burden on the nobility. The high court of appeals in Paris refused to register it, saying that only the chosen representatives of the people in the Estates General had the power to pass

LOUIS XVI

MARIE ANTOINETTE

The Voice of the People
1789

The sun had broken through the clouds after a night of spring showers. Dripping leaves sparkled in the golden light, which flooded the gaily decorated streets of Versailles and the broad terraces of the king's royal palace. It was May 4, 1789, the day of the opening ceremony of the recently elected Estates General.

The streets were crowded with visitors, most of them from Paris, only a few miles away. They had come to see the grand procession of the Estates General and were in a holiday mood. The shops were closed. Local citizens watched from windows, crowded balconies, and rooftops. This was a day, they felt, that would go down in history as the beginning of a wonderful new age for themselves and their country.

The procession moved slowly along the street in the direction of the Church of Saint-Louis, where a mass was to be celebrated. The repre-

new tax laws. The king ordered the judges to register the laws. When they refused, he punished them by sending them into exile in another city. Then the high courts in the provinces protested. They refused to carry on their work so long as the judges were in exile. Since the new laws could not be enforced without the help of the courts, the king and his minister withdrew the new laws and allowed the exiled judges to return to Paris.

This left the money problems still unsolved, and Brienne tried to meet government expenses by borrowing more money. But this, too, required the consent of the high court in Paris. That court would not consent to more borrowing, it said, unless the king promised to summon the Estates General. It took the position that the money problems of France could never be solved without the help of the Estates General, for only that body, representing all the people, had the power to make new tax laws. People of all classes strongly supported the court's view, and raised the cry: "No taxation without representation!"

The fight between the king and the courts went on for many months. Liberals stirred up the people in all parts of France, and the public demand for the calling of the Estates General grew louder. Bankers refused to lend more money to the government, and finally, when the national treasury was empty, the king gave up. He called the Estates General into session on May 1, 1789.

Louis' struggle with the courts was really a struggle with the nobility, for the judges were all nobles, and they were fighting to protect the special privileges of their class. This revolt of the nobles marked the beginning of the French Revolution.

The Voice of the People

sentatives marched by two's, each holding a lighted candle. First came the members elected by the ordinary people of France who made up the middle and lower classes. These were the commoners, usually referred to as the Third Estate. There were more than 550 of them, all dressed in black and wearing three-cornered hats.

Towering above the other marchers of this group was a man with a large head and an ugly face, a nobleman named Mirabeau, who had presented himself as a candidate for the commoners and had been elected as such. Almost all representatives of the commoners came from the middle class, which was made up of merchants, business and professional men from towns and cities. This middle class was called the bourgeoisie.

Next in the procession were the noblemen. They wore wide hats with plumes, silk capes embroidered with gold, tight breeches and stockings of snowy white, with sparkling jewels on their shoes and fingers and swords. Lafayette marched with this group. As an elected representative of the nobles, he no longer felt free to express some of his liberal views, but he was pleased because the people could now speak for themselves through their elected representatives to the Estates General.

Marching behind the richly dressed noblemen came another privileged order, the leaders and priests of the Catholic Church. The priests wore their long black habits, and were followed by the bishops and cardinals in colorful robes. Last of all came the royal family, led by the fat king. Next came the queen, and behind her the king's brothers.

The people cheered and waved as the king passed by, for they were still his loyal subjects. They had been ruled by kings for so many centuries that it seemed natural for King Louis XVI to be the head of their government. But all three orders of society—nobles, churchmen, and commoners—agreed that the king should no longer have absolute power to rule over the people. The time had come, they believed, to place certain limits on his powers. And, since the Estates General represented all the people of France, it could probably force the king to give up some of his powers, and make many other much-needed changes in the government, or so people hoped.

At the same time, each of the orders of French society hoped to use the Estates General for its own benefit. The nobles were very much interested in liberty, but they wanted it mainly for themselves. They had many reasons for being concerned about the future. There had been a time, long ago, when noblemen were the richest and most powerful people in France. They owned the land, and each noble ruled over his

PARISIANS FLOCKED TO CHEER THE OPENING OF THE ESTATES GENERAL.

area of land as though it were a private little kingdom. His farm lands were tilled by serfs, who were really no better than slaves. They and their children had to remain on the land they were working. If they tried to escape, they were hunted down and brought back.

The nobles needed the help of the French king to defend their lands from each other and from foreign enemies. They paid for this protection by sending him money, and men for his army. But gradually the French king had gained control over the lords and taken away much of their power. They were weakened still further when the serfs became free men and were at liberty to leave the farm lands upon which their families had been forced to live for centuries.

Many of these peasants had taken advantage of their newly acquired freedom by moving to towns to work for wages. Some saved enough money to buy land and go back to farming again, but on their own land. The nobles, most of whom managed their estates badly, were usually willing to sell some of their land to raise money. But the more they sold, the less they had left, and the poorer they became. Meanwhile, businessmen in the towns and cities were becoming rich. Advancements in science had made possible the manufacture of cloth and other items much more cheaply than ever before. In addition, France had become a colonial power. Her colonies supplied raw materials for her factories, and provided large new markets for her manufactured goods. As a result, there had been a great increase in business activities during the 1700's, with the profits going to middle-class people of towns and cities—manufacturers, merchants, bankers, and professional men.

Many of these commoners had become very wealthy. Because of their business experience, they were often appointed to important government positions. Some served as ministers to the king. This angered the nobles, who felt that only nobles had the proper qualifications for high government posts. The nobles were alarmed when the king began raising money by selling various government positions to rich commoners. They were even more alarmed when he began selling titles, making it possible for many rich commoners to become noblemen.

The nobles had lost so much of their wealth and influence over the years that the American Revolution and the growing demands for liberty in France frightened them. They realized that all the special advantages they still enjoyed would soon be taken from them unless they fought to protect their interests. They had actually begun that fight with their revolt against the king, which had forced him to call the Estates General.

The nobles expected to control the Estates General, with the help of the leaders of the Church, who were also noblemen like themselves. They wanted the Estates General to protect their special privileges, to provide free schools for their children, and to halt the sale of public offices and titles by the king. They were also going to demand that all important positions in the government and in the army be filled only by noblemen.

Whether the nobles and churchmen, the two privileged orders, could control the Estates General depended upon the method of voting used. In former times, the voting had been by orders— that is, each of the three orders had only one vote. The nobles and churchmen were naturally in favor of this method, for it meant that together they could outvote the commoners two to one.

The commoners had another system in mind. They wanted to vote by head, which meant that each individual representative of each order would be allowed one vote. This method would balance the commoners with the privileged order, because the commoners had as many representatives as the other two orders put together. Furthermore, the liberals in the privileged orders would vote with the commoners of the Third Estate, thus giving them strength enough to control the Estates General.

The commoners felt it was only right that they should have control, for they represented ninety-six per cent of the people. They had been made aware of their importance by many writers. Abbé Sieyès had begun his famous pamphlet, *What is the Third Estate?* with these words: "What is the Third Estate? Everything. What has it been in the political order up to the present? Nothing. What does it ask? To be something."

THE ESTATES GENERAL

Sieyès went on to point out that the commoners of the Third Estate had all they needed to make up a nation. "Take away the privileged orders, and the nation is not smaller, but greater. . . . What would the Third Estate be without the privileged orders? A whole by itself, and a

AS THE MERCHANTS PROSPERED, THEY WANTED A SHARE IN THE GOVERNMENT.

prosperous whole. Nothing can go on without it, and everything would go on far better without the others."

This was the mood of the commoners at the opening session of the Estates General. They felt they had the support of Necker, the King's leading minister, for he also was a commoner. But Necker said nothing in his opening speech to encourage them.

After the first meeting, each of the orders was given a special room in which to check the papers of its representatives. The nobles and churchmen went on to their special rooms and organized themselves as separate bodies. The commoners met in the throne room, but refused to do anything. They were afraid that if they took any action as a separate body, they would be forced into the old system of voting by orders. They argued that the Estates General represented all the people of France, and that therefore it had to meet as one body and vote as one body.

For a month the commoners did nothing. But in refusing to act they prevented the other two orders from going ahead with the business of the Estates General. Privately, some of the commoners urged representatives of the Church to join them, for the church group was known to be the weakest of the three orders.

The Church itself was powerful, well-organized, and owned about a tenth of all the land in France. Although it paid very little in taxes, it often donated large sums of money to the king for the support of the government. It was in charge of all schools in the country, and of relief for the poor. It had its own system of courts, where offenders against the faith could be tried and punished. It had power over the press, since it could decide what should be published. It also kept the public records of all births, marriages, and deaths within the kingdom.

The income of the Church came from its lands and from a church tax, called a tithe, on all farm

WITH NO PLACE ELSE TO MEET, THE COMMONERS GATHERED IN AN INDOOR TENNIS COURT.

products. The peasants who had to pay this tax might not have complained about it so bitterly if most of the tax had been used locally for the parish church and for local welfare and education. Instead, the local priests were given so little that the parishes were always in desperate need. Most of the tax went to central church offices and to the bishops, many of whom lived in princely fashion in Paris, far from the churches under their care.

The men who represented the Church at the Estates General fell into two political groups. The bishops and abbots, being noblemen, shared the political views of the nobles. The parish priests, who were commoners and worked very closely with the people and knew their needs, shared the political views of the commoners. The writer Sieyès pointed out that the religious order was not really a social class at all, but merely a professional group. There were actually only two classes of society represented at the Estates General—the nobles and the commoners.

On June 17, after a few parish priests had joined them, the commoners declared themselves to be the National Assembly. They invited the other orders to join the Assembly, and began acting at once on problems of the day as if they were the representatives of the whole nation.

The bishops and nobles became alarmed and appealed to the king to deal firmly with the commoners and bring them back to their senses. The king decided to do this at a royal session in which the three orders would be brought together so that he could lay down rules for the Estates General to follow.

On June 20, when the commoners gathered at the hall where they usually met, they found the doors closed. They were told that the hall was being made ready for the royal session, but they suspected that the king was trying to put a stop to their meetings. Rain was falling, and they took shelter in an indoor tennis court nearby. There the determined delegates took an oath "never to separate but to meet in any place that circumstances may require, until the constitution of the kingdom shall be laid and established on secure foundations. . . ."

THE TENNIS COURT OATH

The Oath of the Tennis Court, as it came to be called, made it clear that the National Assembly meant to carry on its work, and would defend itself even against the king, if necessary. The commoners were in revolt. They had created a new representative body in which the privileged orders had no special advantages.

Most of the parish priests, as well as a few liberal bishops and nobles, had joined the National Assembly by the time Louis XVI held his royal session on June 23. The king brushed aside all that the commoners had done in the National Assembly. He set up rules for the Estates Gen-

sembly that represented the whole nation. The Assembly changed its name to the National Constituent Assembly, and began writing a constitution for France.

Had the Assembly been able to continue its work undisturbed, it could probably have set up a constitutional form of government under the king without bloodshed. But the king and the nobles had not yet given up. They were determined to prevent the destruction of the privileged orders by the commoners. They must break up the National Constituent Assembly—and to do that, they would have to use force. And, since they could no longer trust the French soldiers, the king secretly sent for units of professional Swiss and German troops that were stationed in other parts of France.

eral to follow, agreed to a few demands of the commoners, but warned that the social orders and the privileges of nobility were not to be disturbed. If the commoners failed to co-operate, he warned, he would dismiss the Estates General. He commanded the orders to separate at once and to begin their work in the three halls assigned to them.

The commoners stubbornly remained where they were, even after the king, the nobles, and some of the churchmen had left. They were reminded by the master of ceremonies that the king had ordered them to leave the hall. Mirabeau spoke for them all, shouting at the top of his voice that they were there by the will of the people, and that they would not leave except at the point of the bayonet. Royal guards were ordered to clear the hall, but a few liberal noblemen convinced them that such action was unwise.

Now it was up to the king to decide whether to crush the rebels or to allow them to have their way. His royal guard could no longer be trusted to carry out his orders. For several days he took no action, for without the help of the guard there was not much he could do. During this time most of the churchmen and some of the nobles joined the commoners in the National Assembly, and finally the king yielded again. He ordered the nobles and bishops to join the others in the National Assembly.

The successful revolt of the commoners had brought into being through peaceful means an as-

The Fall of the Bastille
1789

On Sunday, July 12, 1789, the people of Paris learned that Necker, the popular minister, had suddenly been dismissed by the king. They could only guess at the king's reasons for wanting Necker out of the way. But it seemed clear enough that Necker's dismissal had something to do with the recent arrival of Swiss and German troops in the Paris area. It was said that more troops were arriving every day. Why? People were almost afraid to guess at the answer.

The news of Necker spread quickly, and angry crowds gathered in the streets. A young man named Desmoulins leaped to the top of the table and warned the people to arm themselves. He probably repeated many of the ugly rumors then circulating in Paris. The king was bringing in troops to destroy the Assembly at Versailles. The king had entered into a plot with the nobles to smash the revolution, massacre the patriots in Paris, and become once again the absolute ruler of France.

Desmoulins drew a pistol and waved it above his head. "There is not a moment to lose," he

The Fall of the Bastille

shouted. "We have only one course of action—to rush to arms. . . ."

A growing crowd followed him through the streets. *"Aux armes!"* they cried. "To arms!" A regiment of the king's German cavalry tried to scatter them, and some of the people were slightly wounded. They screamed that they were being massacred, and the crowd became a maddened mob. People armed themselves with sticks and pipes. They broke into the shops of gunsmiths to snatch up weapons. French soldiers left their barracks and joined them. The German cavalry, forced to retreat, hurriedly withdrew from the city. The police had also disappeared, leaving Paris in the hands of the rioters.

Under more normal conditions, the armed citizens and volunteer French soldiers might have been able to keep order throughout the night. But France was then suffering from a serious food shortage. Rainstorms and hail during the summer of 1788 had destroyed most of the grain crops in the countries of western Europe. The crop failure, together with the effects of a world-wide depression, had hurt business in towns and cities and caused many factories to close their doors. The result was that Paris was crowded with an unusually large number of unemployed workers and beggars, all desperate for food. Taking advantage of the confusion, they roamed the streets that night in gangs, breaking into shops to help themselves to food and anything of value they could carry away.

Businessmen and property owners became alarmed and demanded protection. Middle-class people representing the sixty election districts of Paris used the opportunity to set up their own city government, and organized a militia of volunteers to keep order. With an army of their own they could defend themselves against the king's foreign troops, if necessary.

Thousands of volunteers flocked to join the militia on July 13. The king's foreign troops took up positions between Paris and Versailles, thus placing the Assembly in Versailles at the mercy of the king. Paris seemed to be surrounded by troops. Even the cannon on the walls of the Bastille, an old fortress on the east side of town, had been run into position and aimed at the city. During the night, rumors spread that troops were advancing upon Paris from several directions, and panic swept the city.

On the morning of July 14, people rushed to guard the gates of Paris. They tore up cobblestones from the pavements and piled them up in walls or breastworks across the streets to stand off the enemy. Such barricades could be built quickly and they became a familiar feature of street riots during the Revolution. The people wanted weapons with which to defend their city, and they streamed from place to place in search of guns. At the Arsenal, they found nothing. At the Invalides, 32,000 muskets were passed out. Next they went to the Bastille, where it was said that a large supply of firearms was stored.

The Fall of the Bastille

Built originally as a fortress, the Bastille had been a famous state prison for many years. Many tales were told of cruelty and horror within its great gray walls—tales of dark dungeons, of prisoners slowly dying of torture or being eaten alive by rats. No longer a state prison, it was used as an arsenal for the storage of weapons and ammunitions, but its evil reputation lingered on. Its gray rock walls were ten feet thick, with towers almost a hundred feet high. Moats filled with water surrounded the old fortress, making it impossible to reach the courts except by drawbridges.

A committee of three was allowed to enter the Bastille that morning to request arms and ask the governor to withdraw the cannon aimed at the city. The three were well treated and invited to stay for lunch. When they failed to return promptly, the crowd outside became excited and demanded the surrender of the Bastille. Somehow, two men managed to climb the wall and let down a small drawbridge. Angry citizens swarmed over it and into the inner court, while soldiers on the walls above fired down at them. Several persons were killed. The rest retreated, convinced that they had been tricked into entering the court so that they could all be slaughtered.

Everyone in the crowd who was armed began firing at the defending soldiers. In the one-

TIME AND AGAIN IN HISTORY, THE FRENCH BUILT BARRICADES TO FIGHT FOR LIBERTY.

VOLUNTEERS ARMED WITH ANY WEAPONS AT HAND ATTACKED THE BASTILLE.

sided battle that followed, only one of the soldiers was hit. The attackers' losses were ninety-eight killed and seventy-three wounded. Twice during the battle the new city government sent delegates to put a stop to the fighting. But when they approached the fort bearing white flags, they were fired upon and driven back by the soldiers on the walls.

The volunteer city militia and two detachments of French Guards then arrived with five cannon and began firing the heavy guns at the main gates of the fortress. The defending forces might have held out for many hours, but they suddenly became frightened and forced the governor to surrender the Bastille. The big drawbridge was lowered, and the enraged mob rushed in with pikes, knives, hatchets, and muskets, and began slaughtering the defenders. A number of soldiers were killed before order could be restored. The governor was rescued and brought out, only to be killed by a mob on the street. His head was cut off and joyfully carried about the city on the end of a pike.

The Bastille had fallen—and when the people suddenly realized what they had done, they became frightened. They felt certain the king would quickly strike back with his army. One of them later wrote, "We all expected a fight with the regular troops, in which we might be slaughtered." They did not know that the king, too, was frightened. He had lost Paris, and did not have enough troops near at hand to regain control of it. On July 15 he went before the Assembly and said that the future of the nation was now in the hands of the Assembly. He promised to withdraw his foreign troops at once, as he had been requested to do. The next day he also restored Necker to his old position in the council of ministers.

Lafayette, who had recently been made Vice President of the National Constituent Assembly, was appointed to head a delegation that was to carry the good news to the people of Paris. The delegation left at once. It arrived in the city to find a great crowd gathered before the City Hall. After Lafayette had announced that the king's troops were being withdrawn, he learned to his surprise that the people had just elected him commander of the new city militia. Accepting the post, Lafayette raised his sword high above his head and promised to do what he could to save and defend "precious liberty." A way opened before him through the crowd as he walked toward his carriage. The horses had been taken away. The people showed their devotion to Lafayette by picking up the traces of his carriage themselves and pulling him through the streets.

Lafayette later reorganized the militia, which became known as the National Guard. Its colors were red and blue, the colors of Paris. Lafayette added white, the color of royalty, and provided each of his troops with a cockade, or knot, of three ribbons—red, white, and blue. This cockade was adopted by the French as the symbol of the revolution.

The fall of the Bastille, in itself, had no great importance, but to Frenchmen it suggested the end of all the evils they had suffered under kings, and the beginning of an age of justice and liberty. The people of Paris tore down the Bastille stone by stone, as if to make certain of their newly won freedom. To celebrate the event, Lafayette sent one of the keys of the Bastille to his friend George Washington, the President of the United States. The date of the fall of the Bastille, July 14, soon became the great national holiday of France.

THE PARISIANS FORCED THE KING TO LEAVE VERSAILLES AND RETURN TO PARIS.

"The King to Paris!"
1789

In the towns and cities of the provinces, the news of the fall of the Bastille led to wild celebrations and a series of revolts against local governments. These governments had long been unpopular, since most of them were controlled by nobles and others who had bought their government positions from the king. The town people set up new governments, similar to the one in Paris, and organized local units of the National Guard.

The revolution spread to the countryside as well. There the peasant uprising had started even before the fall of the Bastille. The peasants made up at least 75 per cent of the population, and they had been mistreated and abused by the nobles for many centuries. Because of their poor farming methods and the limited amount of land available to them, these farm people were barely able to support themselves, yet they had been burdened with the heaviest tax load in the country. They paid direct and indirect taxes to the king. They paid the church tax. They also paid various fees and rents to the nobles who owned the land. It was true that many peasants were landowners themselves, but even they had to pay fees to the nobles.

Peasants had to serve in the army, and they were required to furnish horses and wagons for the army whenever necessary. They were forced to work on public roads without pay. They were not allowed to hunt or gather wood in the forests. Only the nobles could hunt there—but the nobles could also hunt on lands rented or owned by the peasants. Cattle belonging to the peasants had to be kept at home, but cattle belonging to the nobles could wander about at will over the lands of the peasants, sometimes causing considerable damage. Peasants could seek justice only in courts controlled by the nobles, and these courts always favored the nobles.

These were some of the things the country people complained about, and expected the Estates General to do something about. But when weeks passed and the Estates General did nothing, the peasants became convinced that the nobles had somehow tricked the "good king" into changing his mind. Many suspected that the representatives they had sent to Versailles might even have been thrown into prison.

The peasants believed the nobles had caused the desperate food shortage by buying up grain and holding it for higher prices. They also believed that the nobles had organized the large

925

DÉCLARATION DES DROITS DE L'HOMME ET DU CITOYEN,

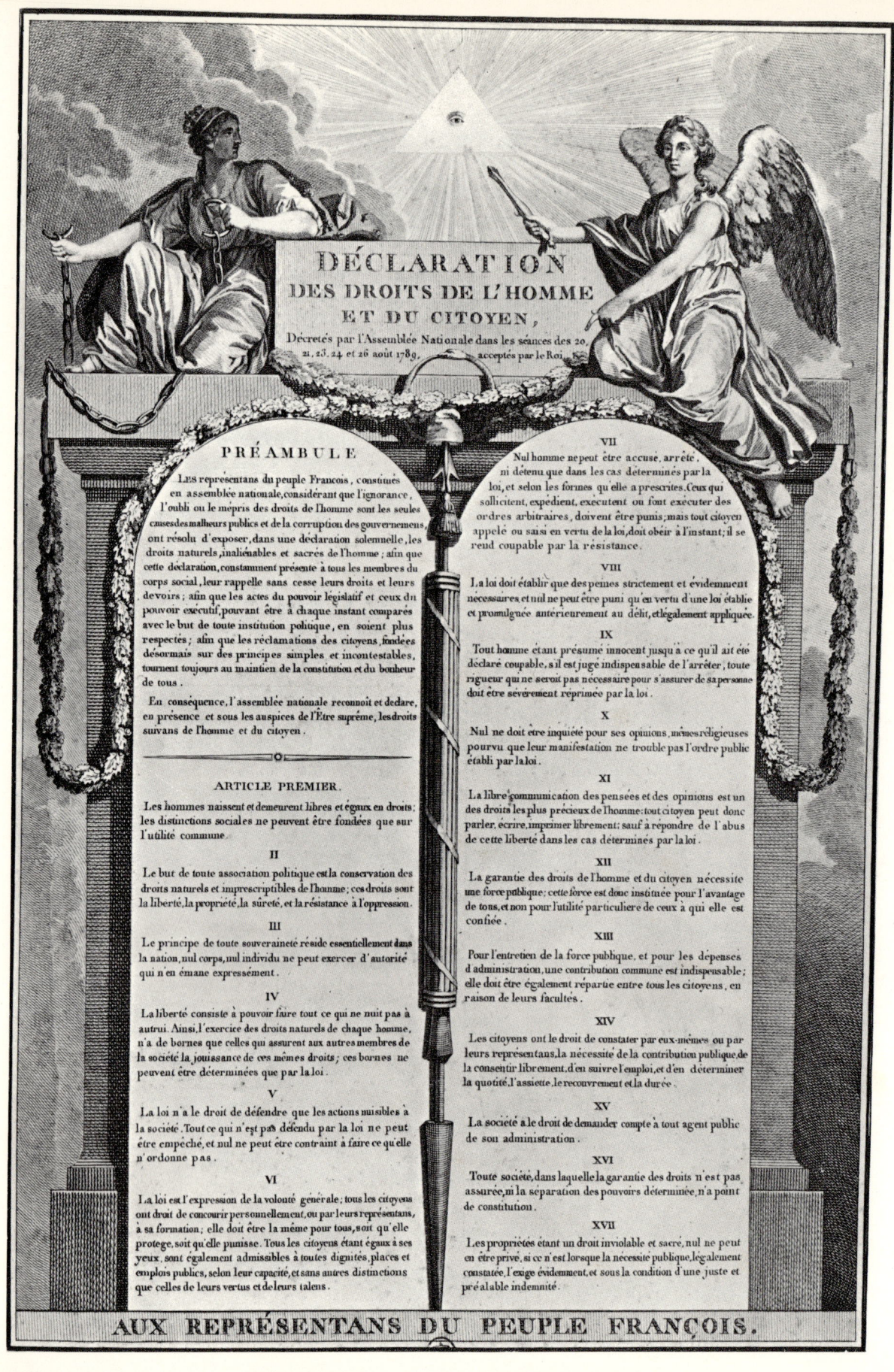

Décrétés par l'Assemblée Nationale dans les séances des 20, 21, 23, 24 et 26 août 1789, acceptés par le Roi.

PRÉAMBULE

Les représentans du peuple François, constitués en assemblée nationale, considérant que l'ignorance, l'oubli ou le mépris des droits de l'homme sont les seules causes des malheurs publics et de la corruption des gouvernemens, ont résolu d'exposer, dans une déclaration solemnelle, les droits naturels, inaliénables et sacrés de l'homme; afin que cette déclaration, constamment présente à tous les membres du corps social, leur rappelle sans cesse leurs droits et leurs devoirs; afin que les actes du pouvoir législatif et ceux du pouvoir exécutif, pouvant être à chaque instant comparés avec le but de toute institution politique, en soient plus respectés; afin que les réclamations des citoyens, fondées désormais sur des principes simples et incontestables, tournent toujours au maintien de la constitution et du bonheur de tous.

En conséquence, l'assemblée nationale reconnoît et déclare, en présence et sous les auspices de l'Être suprême, les droits suivans de l'homme et du citoyen.

ARTICLE PREMIER.
Les hommes naissent et demeurent libres et égaux en droits; les distinctions sociales ne peuvent être fondées que sur l'utilité commune.

II
Le but de toute association politique est la conservation des droits naturels et imprescriptibles de l'homme; ces droits sont la liberté, la propriété, la sûreté, et la résistance à l'oppression.

III
Le principe de toute souveraineté réside essentiellement dans la nation; nul corps, nul individu ne peut exercer d'autorité qui n'en émane expressément.

IV
La liberté consiste à pouvoir faire tout ce qui ne nuit pas à autrui. Ainsi, l'exercice des droits naturels de chaque homme, n'a de bornes que celles qui assurent aux autres membres de la société la jouissance de ces mêmes droits; ces bornes ne peuvent être déterminées que par la loi.

V
La loi n'a le droit de défendre que les actions nuisibles à la société. Tout ce qui n'est pas défendu par la loi ne peut être empêché, et nul ne peut être contraint à faire ce qu'elle n'ordonne pas.

VI
La loi est l'expression de la volonté générale; tous les citoyens ont droit de concourir personnellement, ou par leurs représentans, à sa formation; elle doit être la même pour tous, soit qu'elle protège, soit qu'elle punisse. Tous les citoyens étant égaux à ses yeux, sont également admissibles à toutes dignités, places et emplois publics, selon leur capacité, et sans autres distinctions que celles de leurs vertus et de leurs talens.

VII
Nul homme ne peut être accusé, arrêté, ni détenu que dans les cas déterminés par la loi, et selon les formes qu'elle a prescrites. Ceux qui sollicitent, expédient, exécutent ou font exécuter des ordres arbitraires, doivent être punis; mais tout citoyen appelé ou saisi en vertu de la loi, doit obéir à l'instant; il se rend coupable par la résistance.

VIII
La loi ne doit établir que des peines strictement et évidemment nécessaires, et nul ne peut être puni qu'en vertu d'une loi établie et promulguée antérieurement au délit, et légalement appliquée.

IX
Tout homme étant présumé innocent jusqu'à ce qu'il ait été déclaré coupable, s'il est jugé indispensable de l'arrêter, toute rigueur qui ne seroit pas nécessaire pour s'assurer de sa personne doit être sévèrement réprimée par la loi.

X
Nul ne doit être inquiété pour ses opinions, mêmes religieuses, pourvu que leur manifestation ne trouble pas l'ordre public établi par la loi.

XI
La libre communication des pensées et des opinions est un des droits les plus précieux de l'homme; tout citoyen peut donc parler, écrire, imprimer librement, sauf à répondre de l'abus de cette liberté dans les cas déterminés par la loi.

XII
La garantie des droits de l'homme et du citoyen nécessite une force publique; cette force est donc instituée pour l'avantage de tous, et non pour l'utilité particulière de ceux à qui elle est confiée.

XIII
Pour l'entretien de la force publique, et pour les dépenses d'administration, une contribution commune est indispensable; elle doit être également répartie entre tous les citoyens, en raison de leurs facultés.

XIV
Les citoyens ont le droit de constater par eux-mêmes ou par leurs représentans, la nécessité de la contribution publique, de la consentir librement, d'en suivre l'emploi, et d'en déterminer la quotité, l'assiette, le recouvrement et la durée.

XV
La société a le droit de demander compte à tout agent public de son administration.

XVI
Toute société, dans laquelle la garantie des droits n'est pas assurée, ni la séparation des pouvoirs déterminée, n'a point de constitution.

XVII
Les propriétés étant un droit inviolable et sacré, nul ne peut en être privé, si ce n'est lorsque la nécessité publique, légalement constatée, l'exige évidemment, et sous la condition d'une juste et préalable indemnité.

AUX REPRÉSENTANS DU PEUPLE FRANÇOIS.

bands of beggars that were roaming the countryside. These bands went from farm to farm, threatening to burn farm buildings and to run off the cattle unless they were given food. As spring crops began to ripen in early July, the bands increased in number and invaded the fields to help themselves.

When the peasants heard that the nobles were organizing a large army of beggars beyond the border, they rose up in rebellion. They tore away fences that kept their cattle from grazing on the lands of the nobles. Then came news that the Bastille had fallen. There were wild rumors that starving people in the towns were about to march into the country to help themselves to the standing crops, and that the approaching army of beggars had been paid by the nobles to slaughter the country people. Thinking that they were fighting for their lives, the frightened peasants armed themselves, gathered in mobs, and plundered and burned and destroyed the property of the nobles and the rich.

The local police were helpless. The middle-class people of the towns, unable to protect themselves and their property, called out their units of the National Guard and sent them against the mobs of country people. In the battles that followed, hundreds lost their lives.

The Assembly, alarmed at the violence sweeping the country, held a special session on the night of August 4 to take emergency action. "The people are trying to shake off a yoke which has been over their heads for centuries," explained a nobleman, the duke of Aiguillon. He went on to say that peace could be restored if the privileged classes gave up all their special rights. He then offered to give up all of his rights for the good of the country, but expected to be paid for his property rights. One by one, other nobles rose to follow his example.

A number of decrees were approved to put an end to all traces of serfdom and to wipe out class distinctions. On that night the old order of France came to an end. All Frenchmen were to be equal, subject to the same laws, and were to pay their just shares of taxes. All would have an equal chance to serve in the Church, the government, or as officers in the army. In addition, church taxes and dues were to be done away with, and the Church was to be reorganized.

The Assembly was so pleased with its work that it proclaimed Louis XVI "the Restorer of French Liberty." Next, on August 27, it approved a Declaration of the Rights of Man and Citizen. The Declaration was long and included such ideas as these: All men are born free and remain free, and have equal rights. The aim of government is to protect these rights, which are "liberty, property, security," and the right to fight against unfair treatment. Government is created "not in the interest of those who govern but of those who are governed." A person is free to do anything that "does not harm another." He is free to think as he likes, and has a right to enjoy freedom of press and freedom of religion. A prisoner is to be considered innocent until proven guilty. All persons are equal in law, in public employment, and in taxation.

King Louis did not wish to destroy the privileged classes, and therefore he did not approve the decrees of the Declaration. He resisted them simply by doing nothing about them. The Assembly hardly knew what action to take next. Did it have the right to pass laws without the king's approval? After lengthy debates on the king's veto rights, it decided that he could not veto the constitution or any part of it, but had limited veto rights over ordinary laws. This solved nothing, since he still refused to act on the August 4th decrees or the Declaration.

What was needed to force the king to act, some of the politicians said, was another uprising of the people in Paris. The food shortage was serious again, and there were bread riots in Paris almost daily. But still the people as a whole were not quite stirred up to the point where they would turn in anger against the king. Something more was needed.

That something more was soon supplied by the king himself. He used the bread riots in Paris as an excuse for calling a regiment of soldiers to Versailles. His real purpose, of course, was to be able to deal more firmly with the Assembly. On October 1, a dinner was held in honor of the officers of the regiment. There were toasts to the king, but none to the nation; it was said that the red, white, and blue cockade of the Revolution was trampled underfoot. The people of Paris were furious and threatened to march to Versailles and bring the king back to Paris.

On Monday, October 5, a mob of women appeared at City Hall and demanded bread, and then decided to march to Versailles and see the king. More than 6,000 of them made the long march over muddy roads in the rain. Lafayette followed later in the afternoon with his National

Guard. When he arrived at midnight, the women had already settled down around campfires and all was quiet.

"WE BRING THE BAKER"

Early in the morning, the women and thousands of other persons who had arrived during the night found an unguarded entrance into the palace. Some of them went in to look around, and fighting broke out. Several were killed. The angry mob smashed through doors, and rushed up the broad stairway leading to the queen's apartments. The loyal bodyguard checked their advance just long enough for the queen to escape in a dressing gown to the king's quarters across the hall.

Arriving with his National Guard, Lafayette blocked the way to the royal chambers, and the mob backed away. Not a blow was struck as the people retreated down the marble stairs and out through the splintered palace doors. But once outside, they joined the screaming mob that surrounded the palace. Lafayette finally quieted them by appearing on a balcony with the king and queen and their small son.

"The King to Paris! The King to Paris!" shouted the people, over and over, and they went on shouting until the king agreed to come with them.

That same afternoon, the National Guard led the procession to Paris, with a loaf of bread carried high on a bayonet. They were followed by wagonloads of wheat and flour, the market women of Paris, palace soldiers, and the Swiss Guard. Then came the royal carriage, with Lafayette riding beside it on a prancing white horse. Behind it came several hundred members of the Assembly in carriages, more National Guard units, and more of the people.

"We bring the baker, the baker's wife, and the baker's boy," chanted the people as they marched through the rain toward Paris. They were convinced that having the king and his family living in Paris would mean plenty of bread in the city from then on.

At a welcoming ceremony at City Hall, a red-white-and-blue cockade was pinned on the king's hat. The royal family was then taken to live in the Tuileries, a city palace which had not been occupied by a royal family for more than a hundred years. About two weeks later, the Assembly moved to Paris so that it could be in the same vicinity as the king.

The Revolution seemed to be about over. First, the nobles had revolted, and their victory had forced the king to call the Estates General. Next, the middle-class representatives in the Estates General had revolted to gain control of that body. Their victory over the king and the nobles brought the National Constituent Assembly into being. Then the people in the cities and towns had revolted, gaining control of their local governments. Finally, through the revolt of the peasants, the nobles lost control of the countryside, too. The time had come, it seemed, for the Assembly to continue its work of establishing a free society under a constitution.

The Fall of King Louis
1789-1793

"Down with the King!" That cry was heard again and again on the night of August 9, 1792, as restless mobs gathered in the streets of Paris. They had only one purpose in mind, and that was to make certain the king was toppled from his throne. The Assembly had been warned to dispose of the king before midnight, and that deadline was only hours away. If the Assembly failed to act, the mobs would join forces, march on the royal palace, and seize the king themselves.

As the midnight deadline approached, the frightened members of the Assembly were still in session. It was their duty to protect the king, yet, if they sent more troops to the palace, they could be held responsible for starting a civil war. The Tuileries, as the royal palace was called, was already well guarded by a Swiss guard of 900 troops, about the same number of police, and 2,000 of the National Guard.

The members of the Assembly were troubled by many questions, for France now had a constitution, and the members were the elected representatives of the Legislative Assembly. The new government was less than a year old. Since the king served as the head of that government, what would happen to it if the king were dragged from his throne?

On the other hand, could the new government survive under the leadership of a king who had lost the trust of the people? King Louis had done a number of things which had turned the people against him. It was his threat to use troops against the people that had brought about the fall of the Bastille three years earlier. Then, on the night of June 20, 1791, he and his family had made an unsuccessful attempt to escape from the country. The people had been shocked. They felt the king had turned against them. If he had escaped, he would probably have returned with an invading army to smash the revolution and regain the full powers of his throne. The people, therefore, came to regard King Louis XVI as a traitor. They found it easy to believe rumors that he and other kings of Europe were secretly plotting to overthrow the new French government.

Many nobles and thousands of officers of the French army had fled the country, increasing the fear of war. When it became clear that Austria was building up the forces along the border, France finally declared war, and Prussia soon entered the war on the side of Austria.

THE JACOBINS

King Louis was secretly pleased, for the war gave him new hope. He believed the poorly trained soldiers of the French army would quickly be pushed back. He would then have the opportunity to act as peace maker, and demand the return of all his royal powers for saving France from being overrun by the enemy.

Lafayette, who had been given command of one of the French armies, was also pleased by the war. He knew from his experience in America that men who were fighting for liberty, even if poorly trained, could do well against more experienced soldiers. He honestly expected a French victory, which he hoped would unite the people of France behind their government, and give them new faith in their king and in their constitution. What worried him was that the French were becoming a divided people. In his view, the French revolution had already been won, and now it was time for Frenchmen to support their new government, the king, and the constitution. But most people felt that the revolution had not gone far enough, or that more power should be given the government to protect the gains already won. As a result, Lafayette had lost most of his influence as a leader, while other men, such as Danton and Marat, were attracting followers.

Danton, a Paris lawyer and a powerful giant of a man, had led many street riots. He had fought his way up to a leading position in the city government, and also became a leading member of the Assembly. Marat called himself the "Friend of the People." He was a short, ugly, toadlike man with a limp and a squint, who suffered from a skin disease that required him to bathe in hot water for hours on end. He published the most radical newspaper in Paris.

Marat and Danton were both members of one of the most powerful political groups in France. It was called the Jacobin Club because it met in a building that had once been a monastery of Jacobite monks. In the early days of the revolution, branches of the Jacobin Club had sprung up in most of the towns and cities of France. The Jacobins represented the middle class, and also the workers and peasants. But as time passed, it tended to become more and more liberal, until its members divided into two groups: a radical group that represented the workers and peasants, and a less radical group that represented the middle-class business and professional people. This less radical group came to be called the Girondins, because their most outstanding speakers in the Assembly came from the province of Gironde.

The Girondins, too, were pleased with the war. It gave them control of the government, for the king was forced to appoint his ministers from the Girondins to keep his ministry above suspicion. The radical wing of the Jacobins, on the other hand, was very much against the war. They felt war could only mean defeat for France and more power for the king. They were convinced that the king could not be trusted. He was a danger to the nation, they said, and if the people did not destroy him, he would again become their master.

It was no secret that Danton and the radical Jacobins were planning an uprising against the king. Even the commanding general of the in-

ANGERED BY THE KING'S PLOTTING, THE PEOPLE OF PARIS STORMED HIS PALACE.

vading army, the Duke of Brunswick, knew about it. The duke had so little respect for the French army that he did a very unusual thing. He insulted the French people by warning them not to attack the royal palace in Paris. He said that if the palace were attacked, or the least harm come to any of the royal family, the guilty would be punished, and Paris would be destroyed.

The French were outraged. They took the warning as proof that a secret agreement did exist between King Louis and the crowned heads of Austria and Prussia. The Jacobins boldly accused Louis of passing military information to the enemy. How could France hope to win victory, they asked, so long as a traitor sat on the throne? They did their best to stir up the people. They prepared for the uprising which was to take place if the Assembly failed to act before the midnight deadline on the ninth of August.

On that night, many members of the Assembly were still trying to make up their minds about what to do. As the debate went on, screams from the angry mobs in the streets added to the confusion. Suddenly the clocks of Paris struck midnight. Church bells and drums sounded an alarm throughout the city that the Assembly had failed to meet the deadline, and people poured into the streets, armed with guns, knives, table legs, and long pikes. At City Hall, a group of rebels took control of the city government. Commander Mandat of the National Guard at the palace was tricked into coming to City Hall. On his way he was shot down by a mob in the street. His soldiers fled when they heard the news. Many of them joined the people in their march on the palace.

The royal family and a small gathering of nobles left the Tuileries, crossed a short space of lawn, and took refuge in the meeting place of the

The Fall of King Louis

Legislative Assembly. When the mob arrived at the palace, only the Swiss Guard and a few nobles remained. Someone fired a shot, which was followed by shots from both sides. The Swiss barred the doors of the palace, and fired down at the screaming mass of humanity from upper windows. The people kept coming, and those in front were pushed from behind, pushed into the deadly hail of bullets from the palace windows. Hundreds were killed, and the crowd kept coming on, stumbling over the fallen bodies.

From his seat in the Assembly, King Louis heard the distant sounds of battle. Finally he wrote on a scrap of paper, "The king orders the Swiss to lay down their arms at once, and to retire to their barracks." The Swiss tried to obey, but escape was no longer possible.

The attackers, thinking they had won the battle, smashed down the doors, rushed into the palace, and slaughtered the Swiss with swords and pikes. Everything breakable in the palace was destroyed. Only about one hundred Swiss were alive after the riot, and these were dragged off and thrown into prison. The victorious people celebrated their victory by roaming the streets in mobs, destroying all the statues of Louis XVI in Paris. King Louis never saw his palace again. He and his family were taken to the tower of an old fortresslike building called the Temple, and held there as prisoners.

At his headquarters in the field, General Lafayette still remained loyal to the king. When he was ordered to return to Paris for questioning, he fled across the border, hoping to reach a port where he could sail to America. He fell into the hands of Austrians, who clapped him into prison as one of the leaders of the French revolution.

Lafayette was called a traitor by his enemies in Paris. The Jacobins warned that the country was full of traitors, and everyone who had supported the king was under suspicion. Meanwhile, the news from the battlefront was bad. A large army of Austrians and Prussians had driven back the French, and each new defeat was blamed on traitors within the army. It was rumored that French officers and nobles were plotting with the enemy to defeat France, so that King Louis and his nobles could be returned to power again.

Criticism of the government was made a crime. Every newspaper that did not support the revolution was forced to stop publication. Armed bands were organized to make house-to-house searches for weapons and suspects. The weapons were turned over to the army. The suspects were arrested, and those who resisted arrest were run through with swords or hanged from the nearest lamp posts.

Marat, who spoke for many of the radical Jacobins, wrote in his paper that spies and traitors had to be killed if the revolution was to be saved. "Five or six hundred heads lopped off and you will be assured of peace of mind, liberty and happiness," he wrote. Later, he declared that ten thousand heads would be "barely enough to save the Nation."

Special courts were set up to try suspects. But the trials were too slow to suit the people of Paris. They feared the traitors at home as much as they did the advancing army of the enemy. Marat wanted the guilty ones killed at once. Why should time be wasted trying Swiss soldiers captured at the palace? "What folly it is to even think of trying them!" he said.

The people were frightened and confused. There was no strong leader to guide them, no one to whom they could turn with confidence. The government was weak. Traitors were everywhere. The desperate food shortage was blamed on the enemy, for it was widely believed that the enemy was trying to starve the French to death.

On September 2, word came from the front that the fortress city of Verdun was under attack. It could not hold out for more than a few days at best. And when Verdun fell, the enemy would have an open road to Paris. The people of Paris were warned of the danger by the ringing of church bells and the firing of cannon. Every man and boy strong enough to carry a weapon was expected to join the great army of citizens and march to the front. But the men began to worry about their wives and children. Would it be safe to leave them behind when the city jails were filled with hundreds of people who were dangerous enemies?

Radicals like Marat warned that the king's secret agents would open the prisons as soon as the men left the city, and the streets would run red with the blood of defenseless women and children. The only thing to do was to kill the prisoners now. Kill, or be killed!

Panic swept the city. A cartload of suspects, headed for one of the jails, was set upon by a mob, and the prisoners were torn to pieces. The mob immediately rushed to the nearest prison. Each suspect was identified, asked a few questions, then taken outside to be clubbed and cut to pieces by the waiting citizens. When the executioners had finished their work at one prison, they moved to another, and few prisoners escaped with their lives.

One of the survivors wrote in his diary that at "three in the morning we heard them breaking in one of the prison doors. Our first thought was that they were coming to kill us in our room. Then we heard loud voices from the staircase and realized that they were attacking a room in which a number of prisoners had barricaded themselves. They were all butchered there, as we soon gathered from words and cries."

For four days the massacres continued, and neither the Assembly nor the city government had the courage to interfere. The commander of the National Guard later explained that he had not

THE SEAL OF THE FRENCH REPUBLIC

ordered his men to protect the prisoners because he knew that such an order would not have been obeyed. So the slaughter went on until the people were satisfied that all political suspects—more than eleven hundred of them—had been put to death. Violence spread to many other cities in France after the Paris government announced "that a number of the ferocious conspirators held in prison have been put to death by the people," and recommended that similar action be taken in the provinces.

On the military front, the enemy took Verdun on September 2, and continued on toward Paris. But heavy rains and lengthening supply lines slowed down the advance. Finally, on September 20, the French made a stand on a hill near Valmy. The enemy was forced back and began a retreat to the border. Paris and France were saved.

On the very day of the French victory, a newly elected National Convention held its first meeting in Paris. Its purpose was to write a new constitution for the "Republic of France." The country was never again to be ruled by a king, so the Convention declared. Its representative form of government was to be somewhat similar to that of the United States.

The Convention was faced with the problem of what to do about Louis, the ex-king. They could not very well keep him and his family in prison for life. He could be banished from the country, of course, or tried and punished like a common criminal. The radical Jacobins felt that the country could never be safe so long as he remained in France. They wanted him put on trial and punished. But the less radical wing of the Jacobins, the Girondins, thought the king should

The Fall of King Louis

remain where he was for a while. Arguments for and against trial continued for some time. Then a workman at the palace happened to discover an iron chest filled with Louis' private papers. These papers proved that he had been plotting with enemies of the revolution.

Now even the Girondins had to agree that the ex-king should be tried as an enemy of the state. The Convention heard the evidence in the case and found him guilty. On January 20, 1793, he was sentenced to die within twenty-four hours. The following morning, a cold rain was falling when Louis XVI, in a heavily guarded carriage, took his last ride. Soldiers lined both sides of the street. Behind them crowded the people of Paris, watching in silence as the carriage rolled by. If they were lucky enough to have a clear view, they caught a glimpse of the king's head bent over his prayer book as he read the Psalms of David.

A flourish of trumpets announced the king's arrival at the Place de la Révolution, and the carriage drew up beside the tall beheading instrument known as the guillotine. Thousands of persons watched as Louis climbed to the blood-stained platform. He tried to speak, but could not be heard above the thunder of drums. With help, he removed his brown velvet jacket and his tie, and opened his shirt at the throat so that the blade could cut cleanly. A few moments later, the heavy blade fell, and the royal head of Louis XVI tumbled into the waiting basket. The executioner held up the head so that everyone could see it.

"Long live the republic!" shouted the people. "Long live liberty!"

The king was dead. Some of the people, with tears in their eyes, crossed themselves. Others fought with each other to get bits of his clothing, or to dip their handkerchiefs in the king's blood. One man ripped off the king's bloody shirt and waved it like a flag at the end of his pike. For long years the people had lived under the rule of kings. Now they felt free, and they celebrated by dancing around the guillotine and singing the song of the revolution, the *Marseillaise*.

KING LOUIS XVI WAS BEHEADED ON THE GUILLOTINE.

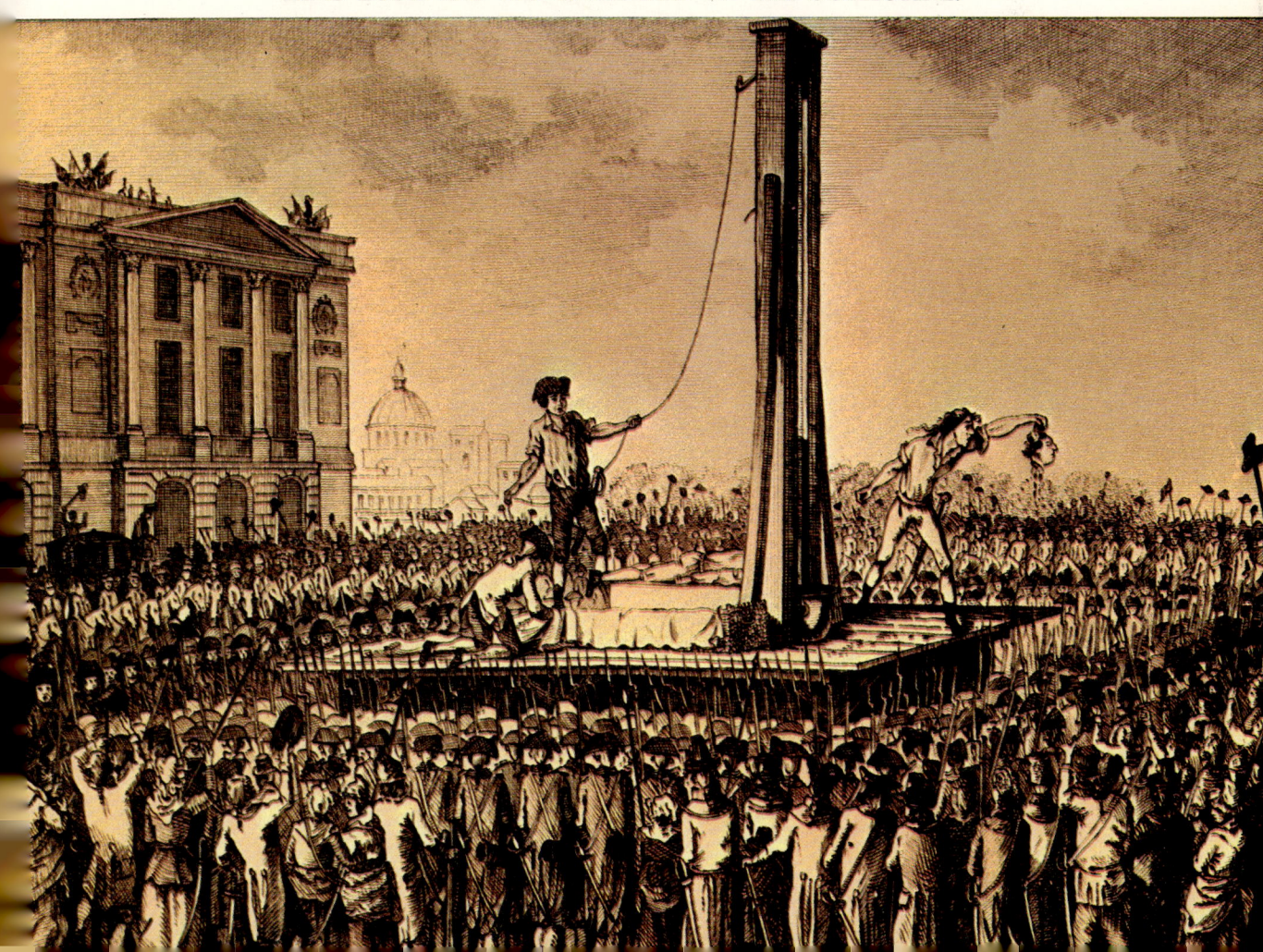

The Terror

1793-1795

The execution of the king stunned the rulers of Europe. They were stunned as well by the French military victories in Belgium and along the Rhine River. Furthermore, the French government was offering to come to the aid of any people willing to fight for their liberty. The revolution threatened to spill over into other countries, becoming a crusade of peoples against kings and nobility. If successful, it could destroy every kingdom in Europe. England and most of the European powers, therefore, joined together in 1793 to crush the revolution and to place another king on the throne of France.

The French attempted to raise a large army to defend the country, but rebellion broke out in a region called the Vendée to the west of Paris. The Catholic peasants of the Vendée turned against the government because it had closed monasteries, taken control of the Church, sold much of the church property, and put to death, imprisoned, or otherwise mistreated many of its priests. The civil war in the Vendée and a number of military defeats at the borders of the country were enough to frighten the French people. There was a serious food shortage again. Unemployment was rising. Prices were going up. Food riots broke out in many large cities, including Paris.

The government was too weak to cope with such emergencies. To provide stronger leadership, a committee of Public Safety was set up to guide the ministers and to serve as the head of the government. Danton was the first Jacobin leader to dominate this committee.

The political group then in power, the Girondins, was blamed for all the ills of the nation. Radical Jacobins demanded the arrest of Girondin leaders. The demand was made again and again without results. The radicals finally stirred up a revolt among the people, surrounded the Convention Hall with troops, and forced the arrest of twenty-nine Girondin leaders. In this way the Jacobins gained control of the Convention.

Many Girondins fled to the provinces, where they organized rebel armies and prepared to march on Paris. These armies won the support of the royalists, the people who wanted a king to be ruler. In addition, the "Royal Catholic Army" of the Vendée had been growing rapidly. By the end of June, most of the provinces and cities of the country were in rebellion against Paris and the Convention.

The Jacobins were desperate. They tried to unite the country by writing a new constitution which favored both peasants and the provinces. The constitution was approved by the people, but was not to be put into effect until after the war was over. The hard-pressed French suffered still another crop failure. British warships added to their problems by blockading their ports. On September 4 came the alarming news that traitors in the French port of Toulon had surrendered the city to the British.

By this time Maximilian Robespierre, a Jacobin leader, had become an influential member of the Committee of Public Safety, and was therefore

CATHOLIC PEASANTS REBELLED AGAINST THE REPUBLIC.

one of the most powerful men in the country. A lawyer from the small town of Arras, Robespierre had been active in the revolution since his town first elected him to the Estates General. He was a small, rather trim person with a weak voice that was difficult to hear in the large auditorium of the Convention. For that reason his speeches were far more effective at the Jacobin Club. He was a champion of the common man, and was probably one of the first to use the phrase "Liberty, Equality, Fraternity," which became the great slogan of the revolution.

The Committee of Public Safety set up special courts to deal swiftly with traitors, and on September 17, the Convention ordered the arrest of all suspects. All enemies of liberty were to be considered suspects. Robespierre felt that all those who were not for the revolution were against it and deserved death. He meant to safeguard the revolution with the blood of its enemies, and this period came to be known as the "Terror."

One of the first important victims of the Terror was the queen, Marie-Antoinette. The charges against her were weak and not very clear, but no one dared raise a voice in her defense at the trial, and she was sentenced to die. She was taken in a crude one-horse cart with a dangling tailgate to the guillotine that stood before the palace that had once been her home. Her hair had turned white, and she was thin after many months in a dungeon. Many people felt sorry for her, but a chorus of catcalls and hoots came from the women of the market place as she passed. When the cart came to a halt, she stepped down without help and climbed the steps of the guillotine. She had nothing to say. Death for her seemed a welcome release from her life in a dungeon.

After the queen had been put to death, the leading Girondins were next on the executioners' list, followed by nobles, military officers, and many others. Over 2,600 suspects were tried and executed in Paris alone, and many thousands more were put to death in the provinces. Civil war raged bitterly for a time. But most rebel armies, untrained and poorly led, melted away as the rebels became discouraged and went home.

CHARLOTTE CORDAY ASSASSINATED MARAT IN HIS BATHTUB.

On the war front, the invading enemy armies had no over-all plan of attack. They refused to fight under one command. The French, led by officers who were young and daring, made the most of the enemy's mistakes, and were soon able to hold the invaders in check. The turning point came when the French recaptured Toulon from the British, with the help of a brilliant young captain of artillery named Napoleon Bonaparte.

After Toulon fell, it was destroyed and hundreds of its citizens were executed as rebels. Marseilles and other rebel cities suffered the same fate. The bloodbath continued without letup, reaching the point where judges were afraid to show mercy. Those who did ran the risk of being arrested as suspects themselves. The extreme radicals carried on a campaign against religion and closed all the churches in Paris. Even Robespierre thought the extremists had gone too far.

But the most radical voice in the land had been silenced by a polite girl from Caen named Charlotte Corday. She believed all the evils of France could be blamed upon Marat and his radical newspaper. She called at Marat's house one evening, gained entrance by saying she had some news to give him, and stabbed him in the chest as he sat in his boot-shaped bathtub.

At her trial, Charlotte Corday said, "I killed one man to save a thousand."

"Do you think there is only one Marat?" a lawyer asked her.

"No, but by killing him I have warned the others. His death will frighten the rest of them." Believing she had done an important thing for her country, she went proudly to her death on the guillotine.

But the Terror continued, and the Jacobin government under the leadership of Robespierre placed the entire population on a war footing. All citizens were required to "discharge their debt to liberty." The army was built up. Factory production was controlled by the government. Prices and wages were fixed.

When most of the rebellions in France had been crushed, and the invading armies had been driven back, Robespierre turned against other leaders of the revolution. Those who were too radical, and those who were not radical enough, were tried and executed. This was a personal struggle for leadership. Robespierre and Danton, for example, were very much alike in their ideas about the revolution and the need for the Terror, but there was not room enough for both of them at the top, and Robespierre was the more powerful of the two. He had his old friend tried and executed, so that Robespierre and his Jacobin followers were left in control of the government and the Convention.

The Terror

Robespierre probably thought of himself as a great humanitarian, a man who had the interests of the people at heart. Almost all government officials were suspected at one time or another of taking bribes, but there was something so sincere about Robespierre that no one ever accused him of dishonesty. He did not seem like the kind of man who could be tempted to do wrong. People called him "the Incorruptible," which suggested that he was a kind of godlike creature who represented the finest qualities of manhood.

And yet this man, whom some historians call a saint and others a devil, was directly responsible for the execution of thousands of people during the Terror. At the same time, he shrank from the sight of blood. He believed the state should not have the power to take human life, but so strong was his faith in the revolution that it seemed perfectly reasonable to slaughter thousands who seemingly stood in its way.

The real goal of the revolution, as Robespierre saw it, was the establishment of an ideal republic based on virtue, or goodness. In this perfect republic people would all be good. No one would be rich. No one would be poor. Instead of jealousy, there would be trust. Instead of hatred, there would be love. Instead of cruelty, there would be justice and understanding. To bring this republic into being, Robespierre felt it necessary to kill off the evil ones. The Terror therefore not only helped France defend herself from traitors, but also paved the way for the ideal republic.

A religion would also be necessary, to hold the people together, but the Catholic religion would not do because too many Frenchmen had turned against it. Robespierre prepared the way for a national religion which would recognize a Supreme Being and the life of men's souls after death. This religion would be tied in with love of country and all the fine ideas of the revolution, such as "liberty and equality." Important dates of the revolution would become religious holidays. On June 8, 1793 Robespierre introduced his new religion in a solemn ceremony in the Tuileries garden. He set fire to figures representing god-

ROBESPIERRE HAD HIS FELLOW REVOLUTIONARY DANTON TRIED AND EXECUTED.

THE CAPTURE AND EXECUTION OF ROBESPIERRE WAS THE START OF THE WHITE TERROR.

lessness, evil, and foolishness, and when these figures had burned down a wooden figure of Wisdom rose out of the ruins.

For several months Robespierre was practically the dictator of France. Now that the country was no longer in danger of being invaded by foreign armies, people began to think about their needs. They blamed the Jacobin government for the shortage of food, for poor business conditions, for the secret police, for the Terror, and for the harsh treatment given the Catholic Church.

To put a stop to complaints, the Convention made it a crime punishable by death for anyone to disagree with the government. The new law caused another wave of executions, known as the "Great Terror," when "heads fell like slates from the roofs." From June 10 to July 27, 1794, some 1,300 people were beheaded by the guillotine. A slip of the tongue, or the lies of a personal enemy, could send a man to his death. No one felt safe, not even the members of the Convention. They suddenly turned against Robespierre and had him arrested, but the radical city government of Paris refused to jail the prisoner.

Early in the morning of July 28, as Robespierre and his friends were planning an uprising of the people against the Convention, government troops broke into their conference room at City Hall. There was a shot, and Robespierre fell across the table with a broken jaw; whether he tried to kill himself or was shot by a soldier has never been clearly established. He and nineteen of his followers were tried and guillotined later that same day.

The death of Robespierre brought about an uprising against the Jacobins. This was called the "White Terror" to show that it was the opposite of the Terror, which was associated with the color red, the color of blood and of the revolution. Many persons were tried and guillotined, and hundreds of Jacobins in the provinces were butchered by mobs. But people began to breathe more easily again. Newspapers began to print what they pleased. They blamed Robespierre for the Terror, and for all the horrible crimes that had been committed while he was in power.

Members of the Convention who had supported the Terror now tried to convince the public that they, too, had been against it. To win public approval, they attacked many unpopular policies of the Robespierre government. The Committee of Public Safety lost most of its power. The Jacobin Club in Paris was closed. Hundreds of prisoners were released from jail. In February, 1795, religious freedom was restored and the churches were opened again. Historians call this period of backing away from the Terror the "Thermidorian Reaction," since it came about in the month of Thermidor, the name substituted for July in the calendar of the French Revolution.

The Convention soon set to work drafting another constitution, which favored the middle class. After it was approved by the people, elections were held, and the new constitutional government came into being on October 27, 1795. The fighting spirit of the revolution slowly died out as middle class people with property came into power. They wanted peace and time to enjoy their newly won freedom. The French Revolution had now run its course.

The Rise of Napoleon Bonaparte

1796-1802

In March of 1796, a new commander named Napoleon Bonaparte was placed in charge of the French army on the Italian front. The soldiers and officers were amazed when they first saw him. He was short, thin, pale, only twenty-seven years old, and spoke French with an Italian accent.

Napoleon was not an unknown. He had first come to public attention as the young artillery officer who drove the British fleet from the harbor at Toulon. Later, as a brigadier general, he had successfully defended the Convention from an uprising in Paris.

What most people did not know was that he had been a rebel most of his life. He had been born on the island of Corsica, a rebel stronghold, where fighting for independence from French rule was considered the duty of patriots. His father had been a rebel leader, and the boy Napoleon had dreamed of the day when he, too, would lead a Corsican rebellion against the French. He had kept that dream alive during his years in French military school, and even after he had become an officer in the French army. During one of his visits to the island, while on leave, he had actually tried to stir up a rebellion in Corsica. The attempt failed, and that put an end to his boyhood dream, but he still remained a rebel at heart.

Napoleon's new army was a small one of only 30,000 troops, and most of them were suffering for want of food and clothing. This was the army with which he was expected to fight the Austrian troops in Northern Italy. According to French war plans against Austria, the Italian campaign was supposed to keep enemy troops busy on the southern front while the main attacks were launched by two large French armies along the Rhine River in the north. These armies were to close in on Vienna, the capital of Austria, from different directions. Napoleon knew these plans very well, but he also had some plans of his own.

"Soldiers, you are half starved and half naked," he told his men. "The Government owes you much, but can do nothing for you. . . . I will lead you into the most fertile plains of the world. There you will find flourishing cities, teeming

THE YOUNG NAPOLEON BONAPARTE

provinces. There you will reap honor, glory, and wealth. Soldiers of the Army of Italy, will you be wanting in courage and firmness?"

Never had the soldiers heard such talk from a general, and they were encouraged. And yet they could not help wondering, for what Napoleon promised was almost a miracle.

Napoleon had something of a miracle in mind. The enemy forces, snug in their winter quarters on the other side of the Alps, would hardly be expecting the French to strike before late spring, after the snow had melted from the high mountain passes. To take the enemy completely by surprise, Napoleon decided to begin his invasion as soon as possible.

THE LITTLE CORPORAL

After a whirlwind of preparations, he led his troops around the southern end of the Alps and northward over the hard winter snow in the passes of the Apennine Mountains. The French cut between outposts of Sardinian troops on their left and outposts of Austrian troops on their right, defeating each in turn. Napoleon fooled the Sardinians into thinking that his army was much larger than it really was, and so forced their king to sign a truce. In less than three weeks he had crossed the mountains and won a kingdom. His soldiers were amazed, and filled with admiration.

Driving the Austrians across the plains of Lombardy, Napoleon won victory after victory. One of his most daring movements was a charge across a narrow bridge at Lodi. His soldiers reported, "It was a strange sight to see Bonaparte that day, on the foot of the bridge, under an infernal fire and mixed up with tall grenadiers. He looked like a mere boy." His soldiers cheered him after the victory and, to show their affection, nicknamed him the "Little Corporal." He entered Milan, the Lombardy capital, in the middle of May. The Austrians withdrew and locked themselves up in the great fortress of Mantua, blocking his way to the east and the north.

By this time Napoleon had become the hero of France. While the French armies in Germany were meeting with failure, Napoleon's series of brilliant victories in the south astonished and thrilled the nation. But high government officials found that his victories in Italy were making him difficult to deal with. They felt it was not good that so much military glory should be reaped by one man, particularly a young man who was leading his first command. They decided to send General Kellermann to Italy to share Napoleon's command as well as his glory.

Napoleon protested in a letter: "Everyone has his own way of conducting a battle. General Kellermann is more experienced than I, and would do it better: but the two of us together would do it extremely badly. I can serve the country efficiently only if you give me your full confidence."

The officials changed their minds about sending Kellermann, for Napoleon did have their full confidence in military matters. What they feared

NAPOLEON'S CHARGE ACROSS THE BRIDGE AT LODI

The Rise of Napoleon Bonaparte

was that he might become so popular that they could no longer control him.

Napoleon conducted a brilliant campaign in Italy, but he enjoyed advantages which made him look better than he was. The generals he faced in battle were old men. One was seventy-two, another in his middle sixties. Still another suffered from gout, and had to be carried from place to place. These generals believed in the old-fashioned rules of war. They advanced toward the enemy with their troops marching side by side in long lines. Napoleon struck at these lines with flying columns. Like an angry bee he charged at them from one direction and then another, breaking up their beautiful formations and causing a great deal of confusion. They never knew what to expect from him next.

VICTORY IN ITALY

The enemy generals complained bitterly. One of them wrote: "This beardless youth ought to have been beaten over and over again, for whoever saw such tactics. The blockhead knows nothing of the rules of war. Today he is in our rear, tomorrow on our flanks, and the next day again in our front. Such gross violations of the established principles of war are insufferable."

Napoleon also had the advantage of a young army and young officers. He could move quickly, and keep the enemy off balance with surprise attacks. For his officers he chose men of great daring. The timid and the slow were weeded out. Those who were fearless in battle were quickly rewarded with promotions. Furthermore, his troops were fighting for a cause. They were fighting not only to defend liberty at home, but also for world revolution.

Napoleon could deliver the message of liberty to the Italians in their own tongue, for that was the language of his childhood home in Corsica. "People of Italy, the army of France comes to break your chains. It is a friend to all the peoples. Have confidence! Your property, your customs, your religion, shall be respected."

With threats and appeals Napoleon soon forced most of the ruling princes and kings of Italy, as well as the Pope, to make peace with him on his terms. From them he demanded large sums of money, libraries, museums, and priceless art treasures, all of which he sent on to Paris as the booty of war.

The fortress of Mantua in Northern Italy held out against the French for more than seven months. Austria made several attempts to rescue the fort, but Napoleon could not be driven off. One of his greatest victories came when he defeated an Austrian army of 50,000 troops at Rivoli on January 14, 1797. The fort of Mantua soon surrendered, making it possible for Napoleon to march on toward Vienna. Unable to stop his advance, the Austrians signed a truce in April, which was followed by a peace treaty a few months later. In this way Napoleon brought his victorious Italian campaign to a close, and his fame had spread to all the countries of Europe.

After a hero's welcome in Paris, he became restless. He could not afford to remain in Paris long, doing nothing, he told his secretary. "My glory is already threadbare. . . . I must go to the East. It is there that great glory can be won." He had a wild dream of becoming another Alexander the Great by carving out a large empire for France in the East.

France was still at war with England, and Napoleon was asked to lead an invasion of the British Isles, but he did not want to give up his dream of conquest in the East. He managed to

The Rise of Napoleon Bonaparte

DEBARQUEMENT DU GÉNÉRAL BUONAPARTE

THIS STAMP COMMEMORATES NAPOLEON'S EXPEDITION TO EGYPT.

convince the government that the best way to strike at England would be to send an army to Egypt, cutting off the British trade route to India. Egypt could also serve as a stepping-stone to India, where France and England were fighting for colonial power.

THE FIRST CONSUL

Sailing from Toulon in May of 1798, Napoleon's army took Malta early in June, then continued on to Egypt. The city of Alexandria fell on June 30. Three weeks later, at the foot of the pyramids, the French won a remarkable victory against the Mamelukes and became the masters of Egypt. A few days later, a large British fleet under the command of Lord Nelson surprised the French fleet lying at anchor in Aboukir Bay, and destroyed it. This naval victory gave England control of the Mediterranean and bottled up the French forces in Egypt. Napoleon was left helpless.

While he and his men were suffering hardships from heat and plague in Egypt, the British landed an army of invasion in Holland. Austria, Turkey, Russia, and Naples also declared war on the French and defeated them on several fronts.

The French were soon forced out of all Italy except Genoa.

When Napoleon heard the news, he turned over his army to his second in command and left it in Egypt. He secretly set sail for home on a small frigate, somehow managing to reach France in spite of the British patrols in the Mediterranean. The French people were happy to have him back in the country, for they felt he brought them good luck. They had lost confidence in the republic under the Constitution of 1795. The leadership of that government was in the hands of five directors, who spent much time arguing among themselves. The result was a weak government. Conditions in France were very bad. Taxes went uncollected, French money lost its

The Rise of Napoleon Bonaparte

value, and unemployment was rising. There was confusion everywhere, and civil war raged in some of the provinces.

Most Frenchmen were neither surprised nor alarmed when Napoleon and several other men overthrew the government. There was no violence. People felt that the old government could not have lasted much longer in any event. It had failed at its job of ruling the country.

Napoleon and his partners presented France with a new constitution on December 15, 1799. It provided for three Consuls to lead the government for a term of ten years. Napoleon was named First Consul, with special powers, and thus became the most powerful man in the country. The new government also had two legislative assemblies, but these could not make law. They could only accept or reject proposed laws sent to them by the Consuls.

To rebuild the nation Napoleon needed a period of peace. He crushed the civil war in France, and made offers of peace to England and Austria. Both countries found his terms unreasonable and turned him down, so again he led an army against the Austrians in Northern Italy. This time he went by way of the high Saint Bernard Pass of the Alps, where Hannibal and his army had crossed 2,000 years earlier. Gun carriages had to be taken apart and carried over in pieces. The guns themselves were lashed to log sleds, each dragged through the snow by a hundred men.

NAPOLEON EASILY DEFEATED A TURKISH ARMY THAT LANDED AT ABOUKIR.

Again Napoleon took the enemy by surprise. He was in the Po Valley before the Austrians even knew he was in Italy. After a few minor victories, he entered Milan on June 2, 1800. Less than two weeks later came the great battle at Marengo. The Austrian army, with more troops and more cannon than Napoleon had, forced the French back, and their defeat seemed certain. But reinforcements arrived in time, and the French won another remarkable victory.

The truce was signed the following day. After still another French victory at Holenlinden a few months later, the Austrians signed a peace treaty in February of 1801. By that treaty the French gained control of most of Italy, and Russia later accepted the peace terms. England defeated the French army Napoleon had left in Egypt, and signed the Peace of Amiens on March 27, 1802.

DICTATOR OF FRANCE

At last France was at peace with all of her neighbors. More popular than ever, Napoleon was hailed as the "genius of war," and the "angel of peace." He won praise even in England, where shops in London sold pictures of him which were labeled "The Saviour of the World." Later that same year the French proclaimed Napoleon Consul for Life. They had many good reasons for their great faith in him. Since coming to power he had built a strong and efficient national government, which collected taxes regularly and gave the people a sound money. He had encouraged industry, reduced unemployment, and established public schools. In addition, he had worked out a whole new system of laws, known as the Code Napoléon, which included many gains of the revolution. It recognized, for example, that all citizens were equal before the law, and that each person had the right to choose his own profession and his own religion.

Napoleon was not a religious man himself, but he won the loyalty of many French Catholics by signing an agreement with the pope. He granted the Church more freedom in France, and, in exchange, the pope gave up all claim to lands taken from the Church during the revolution. Army officers, gathering in Paris after the peace, complained about the religious agreement with Rome and became critical of Napoleon. To win their loyalty, he created a new order called the Legion of Honor, to which he appointed the leading heroes of France. Soldiers honored in this way also received a liberal income from the government. Napoleon's critics soon became his loyal supporters.

Always driven by his hunger for power, Napoleon had a new constitution written shortly after he became Consul for Life. It gave him the power to make treaties, to dismiss the legislative bodies, and to change court decisions which did not please him. He could even make changes in the constitution, with the approval of the senate. And that body was not likely to resist his will, since he alone had the right to choose the candidates to it.

Napoleon had made himself the dictator of France.

THIS OLD PRINT SHOWS NAPOLEON IN HIS COACH.

NAPOLEON CROWNED HIMSELF EMPEROR WITH THE BLESSING OF THE POPE.

Emperor of the French

1804-1815

On December 2, 1804, in a ceremony of great pomp and splendor at the cathedral of Notre Dame in Paris, Napoleon Bonaparte was crowned Napoleon I, Emperor of the French. Pope Pius VII was there. He had come from Rome to offer his blessing, and to place the crown on the head of the new emperor. But Napoleon did not do what was expected of him. Instead of kneeling, he took the crown from the Pope's hands and put it on himself. He also placed a crown on the head of his wife, Josephine.

Only twelve years had passed since the French had risen in revolt against their king. Now, by popular vote, they had placed Napoleon on the throne, and approved a new constitution giving him almost unlimited power. People in other lands wondered if the French were turning their backs on the revolution, but the French did not think so. They looked upon Napoleon as the man who had made laws and treaties to protect most of the benefits which they had won during the revolution.

Yet the French had changed. They no longer spoke of liberty. They were willing to give up some of their freedom in order to enjoy other things that now seemed just as important, and men who had once been great champions of liberty could do little about it. Among them was Lafayette, who had returned to France after several years in Austrian prisons. Not wishing to support a government under which freedom did not exist, he refused to accept any public office and lived the life of a gentleman farmer.

Most Frenchmen simply felt that a practical form of government was more important than liberty. They had discovered some frightening things about liberty during the Revolution—too much of it could lead to wild confusion and mob violence. What they wanted most now was security. Napoleon was a popular leader in whom they

945

had great faith, for he had proved himself as a soldier and as a political leader, and had given them a more dependable government than any they had ever known. They did not think the change they were making was a big one. Napoleon as emperor would continue to give them security. They still had their constitution and their code. France was still to be called the French Republic.

It was a far more efficient government than the old-fashioned royal governments of other European countries. In those countries the royal authority was limited by local traditions, by serfdom, and by special privileges of nobles and churchmen. In France such obstacles had been swept away by the revolution, and Napoleon had organized a government in which all the strength of the nation was subject to his command, even at the local level. He used strong police methods to enforce his will, and would not permit himself to be criticized in books or in newspapers.

TRAFALGER AND AUSTERLITZ

France and England both broke the terms of their peace treaty and prepared for war. France prepared for an invasion of England, building a large fleet of flat-bottomed boats to carry her army across the English Channel. The difficulty was that such a fleet could easily be destroyed by the powerful British navy, and for months the French attempted to lure the British fleet away from the Channel. Waiting at Boulogne on the coast with an invasion army of 150,000 troops and 1,200 boats, Napoleon grew impatient with his admirals. None of them, it seemed to him, were willing to meet the British at sea in a fair fight.

He finally lost his temper when Villeneuve, one of his best admirals, sailed his large fleet of thirty-three ships into the Spanish port of Cadiz to escape from the British. In a letter filled with insults, he ordered Villeneuve to leave Cadiz and face the enemy at once. Villeneuve had no choice. On October 21, 1805, his ships sailed out of Cadiz in a long curved line. Lord Nelson, with a fleet of twenty-seven ships, attacked him in two columns. The Battle of Trafalgar, so named because it was fought off the Cape of Trafalgar, ended six hours later in a splendid victory for the British. Without the loss of a ship, they destroyed or captured more than half the French fleet. They did suffer a great loss in the death of Lord Nelson, who was shot by a sniper's bullet during the battle.

After Trafalgar, Napoleon never again challenged the British at sea, and England's influence was also felt strongly on the continent itself. She persuaded Russia, Austria, Sweden, and Naples to join her in another war against France. They were all convinced that there could be no lasting peace in Europe so long as Napoleon remained in power.

As usual, Napoleon caught his enemies off balance with a series of long, swift marches. Before the Russians and Austrians could join forces, he was able to swing behind a large Austrian army at Ulm and attack it from all sides. The

Emperor of the French

Austrians were forced to surrender. Napoleon then took Vienna, which was not strongly defended, but the city was soon threatened by Russians and what was left of the Austrian army. Outnumbered, Napoleon slowly withdrew from Vienna, making the enemy believe he was even weaker than he really was. At Austerlitz, a place he had carefully chosen for the battle, he took his stand. There he won what he called his "most glorious victory."

The Battle of Austerlitz led to important changes in the map of Europe. Austria lost her possessions in Germany and Italy, possessions which made up a large portion of the Holy Roman Empire. That thousand-year-old empire was broken up, and Francis of Austria lost his right to be called the Holy Roman Emperor. The small German states over which he had ruled were gathered together by Napoleon into a Confederation of the Rhine.

Napoleon was now master of many lands. But as his power grew, so did his dreams of greater glory. He wanted his empire to include all of Europe. One stumbling stone in his path was Prussia, the powerful German state in the north, which was still independent. Napoleon made unreasonable demands upon her, and she joined England and Russia in another war against France.

This war began on October 7, 1806, and Napoleon was well prepared for it. Within a week he had defeated the Prussians in two important battles. After defeating the Russians the following June, he brought the war to an end with the Treaty of Tilsit in July of 1807. The Russians agreed to Napoleon's division of Prussia, one part of which was to become the Duchy of Warsaw, and another part the Kingdom of Westphalia. The Kingdom of Prussia was reduced to a few provinces.

Napoleon crowned his youngest brother,

AFTER NELSON'S VICTORY AT TRAFALGAR, THE FRENCH NAVY WAS NO LONGER A THREAT.

EUROPE AFTER NAPOLEON'S GREAT VICTORY AT AUSTERLITZ

twenty-three-year-old Jerome, King of Westphalia. Jerome was expected to introduce the Code Napoléon and the liberal benefits of the French Revolution to the people of his country. He was supposed to change them from subjects, who knew only how to obey, into citizens who could take an active part in the government of their country.

In one of his letters of instruction to Jerome, Napoleon wrote: "The advantages brought by the Code Napoléon, publicity of legal procedure, and trial by jury, will be characteristic of your monarchy.... Your people must have a liberty, an equality, and a prosperity hitherto unknown in Germany.... What nation would ever wish to go back to Prussian rule when it had once experienced the advantages of a liberal government?"

Napoleon sent similar letters of instruction to his brother Joseph, whom he had made King of Naples, and to his brother Louis, whom he had made King of Holland. In every conquered land and puppet state in the empire, Napoleon introduced his famous code of laws, which offered everybody equal justice under law, freedom of religion, and an opportunity to take part in self-government. Thus, for the middle-class peoples of Europe, Napoleon swung open the door of a promising new world. These people at first hailed him as a hero, a liberator. Later, when they found themselves being used for the greater glory of his empire, as they usually did, their feelings about Napoleon changed.

And, so long as France and England were at war, the peoples of Europe had to suffer for it. The British ruled the seas, and always stood

948

GAINS BY FRANCE

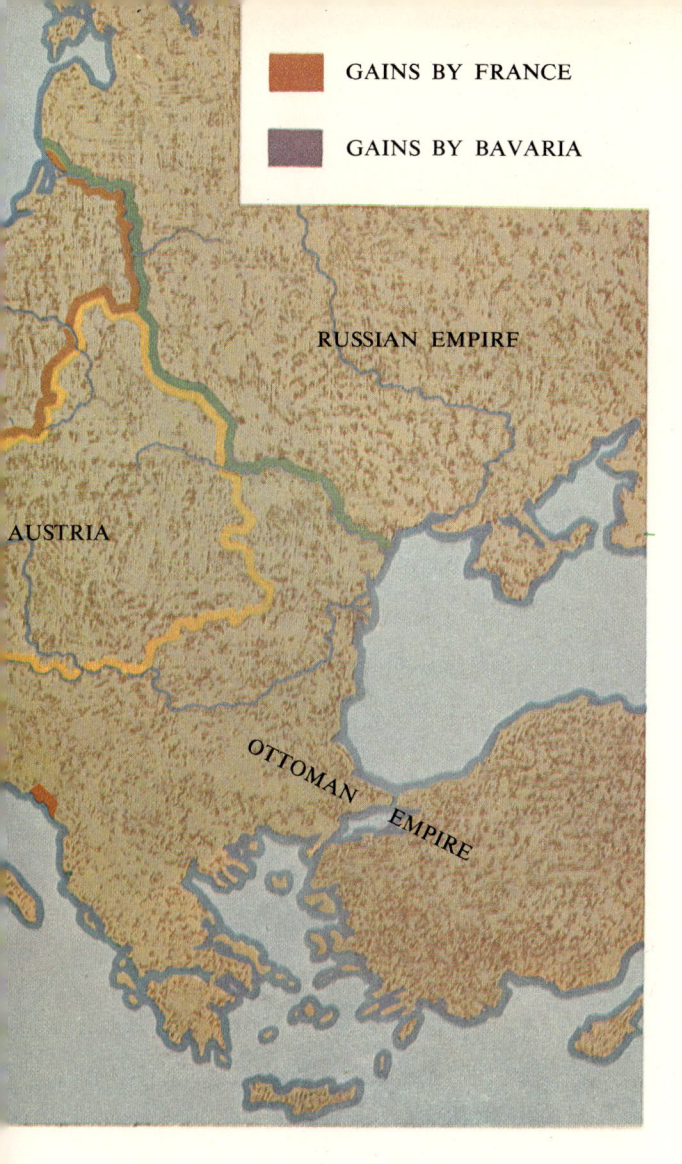

GAINS BY BAVARIA

The entire coast of Europe had to be watched constantly to make Napoleon's action against England effective. He invaded Portugal to close the ports there, and this led to trouble in Spain. When he tried to win control of Spain by placing his brother Joseph on the Spanish throne, the Spaniards rose up in revolt. To make matters worse, England sent an army to help the Spanish rebels. Bands of Spanish guerillas struck and melted away to strike again, pinning down some of the finest troops of France.

The fighting spirit of the rebels amazed and encouraged other peoples of Europe. What was happening in Spain proved that Napoleon's troops were only human, after all. They could be beaten. The Austrians were so encouraged that they made war on France once again—and again suffered defeat at the hands of Napoleon.

During 1810 and 1811, the fighting went on in Spain, but Napoleon controlled most of Europe. The Continental System had become a serious problem. By preventing the normal flow of commerce between countries, it created poor business conditions, high prices, and much unemployment everywhere in Europe. Furthermore, the French were tired of war. So were the other peoples of Europe. Moreover, they were tired of their French masters. The ideas of human rights and liberty that were so much a part of the French Revolution had given people the feeling of independence and increased their national pride; now they were becoming restless, and difficult for France to control.

ready to aid any European country bold enough to make war on France. Napoleon could not strike back at England directly. The best he could do was to close all ports under his control to British shipping. This included all ports in Prussia, Holland, Belgium, France, Italy, and Spain. The Danes were willing to co-operate, and the Russians had also agreed to do so in the Treaty of Tilsit.

Napoleon called his plan the Continental System. He believed that if he could take all European markets away from British manufacturers, he could force England to sign a treaty. But England turned the tables by declaring a blockade of all ports under French control, turning back the ships of all nations. The Continental System caused great suffering and hardship on both sides of the Channel.

THE INVASION OF RUSSIA

Russia and France, both guilty of treaty violations, prepared to go to war in the spring of 1812. This war was part of Napoleon's larger plan for gaining control of all Europe, but he had a number of reasons for fighting Russia. The Russians had opened their ports to British trade, thus destroying the effect of Napoleon's Continental System. Napoleon and Alexander of Russia also had serious differences over Poland and the Turkish Empire. Russia was supported in her war effort by England and Sweden, and Napoleon raised a gigantic army of more than 500,000 troops, which included Italians, Poles, Swiss, Dutch, Germans, and Spaniards. He hoped this large army would strike terror in the Russians and so bring them quickly to the point of surrender. But the huge size of the army actually

Emperor of the French

made it slow and awkward, and almost impossible to feed.

The Russians were so greatly outnumbered that they backed away as Napoleon advanced into Russia. Again and again the Russians avoided battle, burning villages and crops as they fell back, leaving only barren land in which the French could find neither food nor shelter. As the French marched deeper and deeper into the country, they outran their food supplies. Tens of thousands fell behind, too weak to continue.

When Napoleon reached Moscow on September 13, he found it an almost deserted city. The following day mysterious fires broke out in all parts of the city, destroying most of it. For a month Napoleon awaited an offer of peace from Alexander, and finally he had no choice but to make the long march back to France. It began on October 19, and the Russians and the weather combined to make it the most costly retreat in all history. The French troops were tormented almost daily by surprise attacks of mounted Cossacks, but it was the deep snow and the bitter cold of the Russian winter that turned retreat into catastrophe. There was no help for those who weakened and fell. In a few minutes they were nothing more than frozen lumps in the drifting snow. The wolves that followed behind usually found them before the Russians did.

RETREAT AND EXILE

Like ghosts in rags, the French army stumbled on and on through the snow. Many threw their muskets away. In the last week of November they came to the Berezina River and found the bridge destroyed, while on the far bank of the river a large Russian army waited for them. Napoleon fooled the Russians into thinking he intended to cross at another place. While the Russian army marched away, the French engineers quickly built two bridges. Most of the French had crossed before the Russians discovered they

NAPOLEON'S RETREAT FROM MOSCOW WAS A DISASTER FOR THE FRENCH ARMY.

had been tricked and came rushing back. But once again the French losses were staggering. By the time the Grand Army had reached the border of Russia on December 18, it had been reduced to 18,000 men.

Napoleon could not hide the fact that his Russian campaign had been a tremendous and costly blunder. People began to say that his luck had run out, and his enemies prepared to strike before he could regain his strength. In desperate haste, Napoleon began building a new army. Many of his recruits were no more than boys. He did not have time to train them, for large armies of Prussian patriots were already threatening in the north. Prussia, England, Sweden, and Austria also joined in the war against France.

Even though the new French army was short of cannon and other weapons, Napoleon managed to win several battles. But at Leipzig his German troops from Saxony and Württemberg deserted him, reducing his army to 40,000 troops. He was forced to give up the city, and fall back to the Rhine in his first great defeat. The invasion of France took place that winter, and Napoleon could not stop it. Paris fell to the enemy on March 21, 1814, and less than two weeks later Napoleon was forced to give up his throne. He was sent to the little island of Elba, off the coast of Italy, to live there in exile for the rest of his life.

Napoleon was joined by his mother and sister. "He seems to have forgotten the past," wrote one of his friends. "The management of his small household gives him occupation; he is now looking out for a suitable site to build his country-seat; we ride, and drive, and sail round the coasts as much as we please." A year later, however, all Europe was shocked when Napoleon escaped from the island. Landing in France, he began a triumphant march toward Paris to rescue the nation from its weak and unpopular king, Louis XVIII.

THE BATTLE OF WATERLOO

King Louis had kept many of the changes brought about by the revolution. He had given the French a representative form of government much like the one in England. But he had retired most of Napoleon's army officers on half pay and appointed nobles in their place. Now the nobles were demanding many of their old privileges, including the return of property which had been taken from them and sold to the peasants during the revolution. Word of this had reached Napoleon and made him decide the time had come to return to France. And, indeed, the peasants welcomed him, and many joined him on his march toward Paris.

But a Paris newspaper reported, "The monster has escaped from his place of exile!" And King Louis sent troops to arrest him. When Napoleon met them on the road near Grenoble, he recognized many men who had served under him. He quickly leaped from his horse, threw open his cloak and said, "If there is one amongst you who wishes to kill his emperor, let him come forward and do so. Here I am!"

No one moved. After a silence that seemed endless, one of the soldiers shouted, "Long live the Emperor!" With cries of joy, the soldiers joined their emperor on his march to Paris.

The march took twenty days. Fat King Louis fled from the country, and Napoleon took back his throne without firing a shot. His first act was to appeal to the other countries for peace, but they refused to trust him. Once again Russia, Austria, Prussia, and England made ready to invade France. Napoleon saw that he needed a quick victory to win the full support of his countrymen and divide his enemies. He marched his troops into Belgium, met the Prussians, and drove them back before they could join the British and other forces under General Wellington.

At noon on June 18, 1815, he attacked Wellington, who held a position on a hill near the town of Waterloo. Napoleon saw no reason to be concerned. The British outnumbered him slightly, but he did not respect them as soldiers. His one fear was that Wellington might try to escape. He did not know that the Prussian army was only hours away, and hurrying west to join Wellington. Earlier he had sent his own General Grouchy with 30,000 troops to chase the Prussians east and to prevent them from coming to Wellington's aid, but Grouchy had been unable to find them.

The battle was several hours old and the British had beaten back several French attacks when Napoleon heard that the Prussians were coming in force. He sent a note by messenger to Grouchy, ordering him to come back at once, but Grouchy was many miles away. Now he had to beat the English quickly before the Prussians arrived. He ordered a great cavalry charge against the English center, but it stood firm. He still kept his old guard, his best soldiers, ready to send in if the enemy showed signs of weakening. Napoleon held them back until just after dusk, when the Prussians came up and launched an attack on his right flank. His old guard went in, but it was too late. The French broke in panic, and Napoleon and his men fled for their lives.

THE TREATY OF VIENNA

The defeat at Waterloo, one of the most important battles in history, cost Napoleon his throne. After an unsuccessful attempt to escape to the United States, he gave himself up to the British and was sent to Saint Helena, an island in the South Atlantic. There he lived in exile until his death on May 5, 1821.

With Napoleon removed from Europe, the great powers tried to establish a lasting peace with the Treaty of Vienna in 1815. The Netherlands, Switzerland, and Sardinia were to serve as buffer states between the big countries—Russia, Austria, Prussia, and France. France was to be occupied for a time, and her boundaries were cut back to about the same as they had been in 1789. Austria won control of Italy again, and shared influence over the German states with Prussia.

King Louis returned to his throne in France, but neither he nor his nobles ever succeeded in turning back time. The revolution, with the help of Napoleon, had left its mark not only upon France, but upon Europe and the world. The Code Napoléon continued as the basic system of laws in France and served as a model for the law makers of many lands, including Holland, Italy, Spain, parts of Germany, South America, and the state of Louisiana in the United States.

Historians look upon the French revolution as the great turning point in modern history. It multiplied the effects of the American Revolution many times over. It led people to discover the great strength of their numbers, and prompted them to use that strength against special privilege and the absolute rule of kings. It also led people to discover the ideal of nationalism, of people united and working together for the good of their country. It would inspire many revolutions in many lands, where once again men would raise the slogan first used by the French—"Liberty, Equality, Fraternity."

NAPOLEON'S DEFEAT AT WATERLOO ENDED FOREVER HIS HOPES FOR CONQUEST.

IMPORTANT DATES AND EVENTS IN

1792 Austria and Prussia form an alliance against France; the king is arrested and France declared a republic; the Assembly calls a National Convention.

1793 The king is tried and executed for treason; England, Spain and Holland join the alliance against France; Robespierre gains power; the reign of terror begins.

1794 The Terror continues until a coup by moderates brings about the fall of Robespierre and suppression of the political rights of the Jacobins.

1795 The White Terror against radicals begins; Prussia withdraws from the war against France.

1796-1797 Napoleon Bonaparte leads a French army into Italy and defeats the Austrians.

1798-1799 Hoping to cut England off from India, Napoleon lands in Egypt.

1798 England and Russia form a new alliance against France and are later joined by Austria.

1799 Napoleon returns from Egypt and overthrows the Directory, becoming the first consul and dictator.

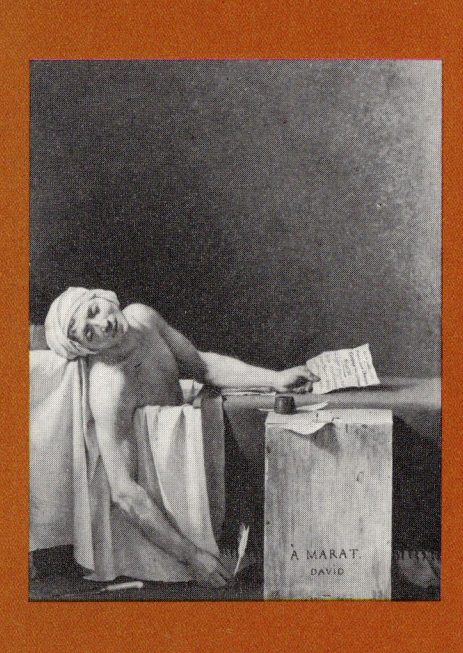

THE AGE OF REVOLUTION 1792-1815

1802 Peace with England; Napoleon becomes consul for life.
1803 England again declares war on France.
1804 Napoleon is crowned emperor of the French.
1805 Austria, Russia, Sweden declare war on France; Nelson destroys the French fleet at Trafalger; Napoleon defeats the Austrian and Russian armies at Austerlitz; Austria makes peace with France.
1808 Napoleon invades Spain and makes his brother king; the Spanish, aided by England, revolt.
1809 Austria declares war on France; Napoleon defeats them and captures Vienna.
1812 Napoleon's invasion of Russia ends in a retreat in which most of the army is lost.
1813 Prussia and Austria declare war on France.
1814 The allies invade France and capture Paris, exiling Napoleon to the island of Elba.
1815 Napoleon lands in France and raises an army; he is defeated at Waterloo and exiled to St. Helena, where he later dies.